One Bill Away

When a Hospital Bill Becomes a Financial Disaster

Author - Shailesh Shah

About the Author

Shailesh Shah is a seasoned insurance and financial services professional with over two decades of experience across banking, life insurance, and health insurance sectors. Throughout his career, he has worked with reputed organizations including Bajaj Allianz Life Insurance, ICICI Bank, HDFC Bank, and Star Health Insurance.

Having interacted with thousands of families, salaried professionals, business owners, and insurance advisors, he has witnessed firsthand how a single medical emergency can create significant financial stress for even the most disciplined savers. His extensive experience in customer advisory, insurance planning, claims support, and financial protection has given him deep insights into the challenges faced by Indian families when dealing with healthcare expenses.

Today, through training, consulting, and awareness initiatives, he is committed to helping individuals make informed financial decisions and build stronger financial protection systems for their families.

Why This Book Was Written

Over the years, I have met countless families who believed they were financially secure until a medical emergency changed everything.

Many people spend years building savings, investing for their children's education, purchasing homes, and planning for retirement. Yet one unexpected hospitalization often wipes out years of hard-earned wealth within a matter of days.

The sad reality is that most people buy health insurance without fully understanding what they are purchasing. They focus on premium amounts instead of coverage, ignore policy conditions, misunderstand claim procedures, and often discover policy limitations only during a medical crisis.

This book was written to bridge that knowledge gap.

My objective is simple: to help every Indian family understand health insurance in practical, easy-to-understand language so they can make informed decisions before a medical emergency occurs.

Lessons From My Experience

During my journey in the insurance industry, I have seen both sides of the story.

I have witnessed families who recovered from major health challenges without financial stress because they had the right insurance protection. At the same time, I have seen families forced to break fixed deposits, sell investments, borrow money, or take loans because their insurance coverage was inadequate or poorly structured.

These experiences taught me an important lesson:

Health insurance is not merely a financial product. It is a financial protection tool that safeguards a family's future, dreams, and peace of mind.

The knowledge shared in this book comes not only from industry experience but also from real-life customer interactions, claim situations, underwriting challenges, and practical problem -solving that I have encountered throughout my career.

What You Will Learn From This Book

This book is designed to help you:

• Understand the real financial impact of medical emergencies.

• Learn why healthcare costs are rising rapidly in India.

• Choose the right health insurance coverage for your family.

• Understand policy terms, exclusions, waiting periods, and fine print.

• Avoid common mistakes that lead to claim rejections.

• Master cashless and reimbursement claim processes.

• Build a strong insurance protection strategy using base plans, super top-ups, and riders.

• Create a long-term health insurance framework that grows with your family's needs.

A Final Message

Health insurance cannot make you rich.

But it can prevent you from becoming poor because of a medical emergency.

The purpose of this book is not to sell insurance. It is to empower you with knowledge so that you can make better decisions, protect your family's financial future, and face medical uncertainties with confidence.

If this book helps even one family avoid financial hardship during a health crisis, its purpose will have been fulfilled.

Let us begin this journey toward financial protection, awareness, and peace of mind.

Disclaimer :-

This book is intended for educational and awarcness purposes only. Insurance products, policy terms, premiums, and regulations may change over time. Readers should consult licensed insurance advisors and policy documents before making financial decisions.

Tax laws, insurance regulations, policy features, and healthcare costs may change over time. Readers are advised to verify the latest provisions from official sources before making financial or insurance-related decisions.

Book Summary :-

This book is a practical, no-nonsense guide that shows Indian middle-class and upper middle class families, salaried professionals, and small business owners exactly how one medical emergency can wipe out a decade of savings and how to prevent it.

It simplifies health insurance in clear, actionable language, demystifying policies, fine print, and claims so readers can buy right and claim right. Readers will finish with a Step-by-step protection plan right sum insured, right policy structure, and right claims strategy so hospital bills never derail their financial future. The transformation is from anxious, underinsured, and exposed to confident, protected, and financially resilient.

This Book Is For:

✓ Salaried Employees

✓ Business Owners

✓ Parents

✓ Young Professionals

✓ Insurance Advisors

✓ Mutual Fund Distributors

✓ Financial Planners

✓ Anyone Responsible for Family Finances

"After reading this book, readers will know exactly how much health insurance they need, which policy structure to choose, and how to avoid the mistakes that cause claim rejections."

Chapter 1

The Unseen Threat to Middle-Class Wealth

(Part I)

It was 2:07 a.m. when Ramesh's phone rang.

No one expects good news at that hour.

Half asleep, he reached for his phone and saw his younger brother's name flashing on the screen. Before he could ask a question, he heard panic on the other side.

"Papa has been admitted to the ICU. Come immediately."

Within minutes, Ramesh was driving through empty streets toward the hospital. His mind raced through possibilities. Heart attack? Stroke? Accident? He did not know.

When he reached the hospital, doctors were already attending to his father. Family members sat silently outside the ICU. Some prayed. Others stared blankly at the floor.

Like every son, Ramesh's first concern was his father's health.

His second concern arrived a few minutes later.

The hospital administrator handed him an estimate.

The expected treatment cost was between 8 lakh to 12 lakh.

In that moment, a new fear entered the room.

The medical crisis had become a financial crisis.

The Illusion of Security

Ramesh was not poor.

He worked for a respected company. He owned an apartment. He had investments in mutual funds. He maintained a fixed deposit and contributed regularly toward retirement.

By every traditional definition, he was financially responsible.

Yet standing outside that ICU, he realized something important.

There is a difference between building wealth and protecting wealth.

Most middle-class families spend decades learning how to earn money, save money, and invest money.

Very few spend time understanding how quickly wealth can disappear.

The New Middle-Class Dream

India's middle class has transformed dramatically over the past two decades.

Previous generations measured success differently.

A secure government job.

A modest home.

Basic education.

Simple retirement.

Today's middle class dreams much bigger.

Children attend premium schools.

Families purchase homes through long-term loans.

International vacations are no longer unusual.

Technology, lifestyle upgrades, and aspirations continue growing.

This progress is inspiring.

But it also creates vulnerability.

Modern families often carry multiple financial responsibilities simultaneously.

Home loans.

Car loans.

Children's education.

Retirement planning.

Support for aging parents.

Business investments.

Monthly expenses.

A major health event can place pressure on all of them at once.

The Problem Nobody Talks About

When people discuss financial planning, they usually focus on investments.

Mutual funds.

Stocks.

Real estate.

Retirement planning.

Tax saving.

Healthcare planning rarely receives the same attention.

Ironically, healthcare risk has the power to destroy every other financial goal simultaneously.

A market correction may reduce wealth temporarily.

A medical emergency can force immediate liquidation.

That difference matters.

The Story of the Deshmukh Family

Several years ago, I met a family in Pune who appeared financially secure.

Mr. and Mrs. Deshmukh were both working professionals.

They had a home, a growing investment portfolio, and a clear financial plan.

Their goals were straightforward.

Fund their daughter's higher education.

Pay off their housing loan.

Build a comfortable retirement corpus.

Everything seemed on track.

Then Mrs. Deshmukh received unexpected news.

She was diagnosed with breast cancer.

The diagnosis changed everything.

Initially, the family focused only on treatment.

Doctors.

Hospitals.

Tests.

Treatment plans.

Second opinions.

The emotional impact was overwhelming.

But another reality emerged slowly.

The financial impact.

Over the next several months, expenses extended far beyond hospital bills.

Specialized investigations.

Travel expenses.

Follow-up consultations.

Medicines.

Supportive therapies.

Additional caregiving requirements.

Some costs were insured.

Others were not.

The family eventually redeemed investments originally meant for their daughter's education.

Retirement contributions stopped temporarily.

Planned financial goals were delayed.

Thankfully, Mrs. Deshmukh recovered.

The family recovered too.

But rebuilding their finances took years.

The Real Meaning of Financial Risk

Many people assume financial risk means losing money in the stock market.

Healthcare introduces a different kind of risk.

Market losses are usually visible.

Medical risk is invisible.

You cannot predict exactly when illness will arrive.

You cannot schedule an emergency.

You cannot negotiate with a diagnosis.

That uncertainty makes healthcare risk uniquely dangerous.

The ₹10 lakh. Illusion

During financial planning discussions, people often tell me:

"I have ₹10 lakh. saved."

At first glance, that sounds reassuring.

But let us examine it more closely.

Suppose a serious illness requires treatment costing 8 lakh.

Immediately, 80% of those savings disappear.

If additional follow-up treatment is required, the remaining amount may disappear too.

What looked like financial strength yesterday suddenly becomes financial fragility.

The issue is not whether savings are important.

They are essential.

The issue is assuming savings alone are enough.

Why Healthcare Costs Feel Different

Most purchases create value.

A home creates an asset.

Education creates opportunity.

Investments create future wealth.

Medical expenses are different.

Families spend money because they have no choice.

No one plans a heart attack.

No one budgets for cancer.

No one schedules an ICU admission.

This is why healthcare costs feel emotionally different from almost every other expense.

The Emotional Cost Nobody Measures

Financial planners can calculate expenses.

Hospitals can calculate bills.

Accountants can calculate losses.

But some costs never appear in spreadsheets.

Stress.

Fear.

Anxiety.

Relationship strain.

Sleepless nights.

Emotional exhaustion.

During serious illness, families often experience all of them simultaneously.

These invisible costs rarely receive attention, yet they affect decision-making profoundly.

What Wealth Really Means

Many people define wealth as accumulated assets.

A larger house.

More investments.

Higher income.

But after speaking with thousands of families over the years, I have come to a different conclusion.

True wealth is not measured only by what you own.

It is measured by your ability to withstand unexpected events without destroying your future.

A family with moderate wealth and strong protection may be more secure than a wealthy family with no protection strategy.

That distinction is critical.

A Question Every Family Must Answer

Imagine receiving a call tonight.

A parent has been hospitalized.

A spouse requires emergency surgery.

A child needs urgent medical treatment.

What would happen financially?

Would savings be enough?

Would investments need to be redeemed?

Would education goals be affected?

Would retirement plans be delayed?

Would loans become necessary?

Most families never ask these questions.

Yet answering them honestly may be one of the most important financial exercises they ever perform.

Closing Thought

The greatest threat to middle-class wealth is not always poor investing.

It is not always unemployment.

It is not always economic recession.

Sometimes it is a hospital bill.

A single event.

A single diagnosis.

A single unexpected night that changes everything.

The families who understand this reality early gain something invaluable.

Time to prepare.

And in financial planning, preparation is often the difference between a setback and a catastrophe.

Part II

How One Medical Emergency Can Destroy Years of Hard Work

The Three Buckets of Wealth Destruction

When people think about a medical emergency, they usually think about one thing: the hospital bill. However, after spending decades interacting with families across different financial backgrounds, I have learned that hospital bills are often only the beginning of the financial damage.

A serious illness usually attacks a family's finances through three separate buckets:

1. Direct Medical Expenses
2. Loss of Income
3. Destruction of Future Financial Goals

Most families prepare for the first bucket. Very few prepare for the second and third.

Bucket One: Direct Medical Expenses

Hospitalization, ICU charges, specialist consultations, surgeries, medicines, diagnostics, and follow-up treatment can consume years of savings within weeks. A retirement corpus may take twenty years to build but can disappear in a matter of days during a major health crisis.

Bucket Two: Loss of Income

Imagine a business owner who spends three months recovering from surgery. The hospital bill may be covered, but who compensates for lost customers, missed opportunities, and reduced productivity?

For self-employed professionals, consultants, distributors, advisors, doctors, and trainers, illness can immediately affect earnings.

Bucket Three: Destruction of Future Goals

A medical emergency rarely pays for itself. Money usually comes from somewhere:

- Children's education fund
- Retirement corpus
- Mutual funds
- Fixed deposits
- Business expansion capital

The crisis gets solved. The future quietly pays the price.

The Story of Aarav

Aarav was nine years old when a sudden medical condition required emergency hospitalization.

His parents had spent years building an education fund. Every month, they invested systematically because they wanted to provide the best opportunities for their son.

When the hospitalization occurred, nothing mattered except Aarav's recovery.

The treatment succeeded.

Months later, the parents realized their education corpus had been exhausted.

The illness was temporary.

The financial impact lasted much longer.

The School Principal

A 52-year-old school principal diagnosed with kidney failure.

- Treatment started.
- Dialysis twice weekly.
- Son's MBA fund used.
- Retirement postponed by 5 years.

The Day Everything Changed for Sandeep

Sandeep was forty-five years old and considered himself healthy. Long work hours and stress had become normal parts of life.

One morning he suffered a major cardiac event.

The surgery was successful.

The challenge came afterward.

Working hours reduced.
Travel became restricted.
Income growth slowed.
Future plans required adjustment.

Years later he would say:

"The surgery cost money. The recovery cost opportunities."

The Hidden Costs Nobody Calculates

Families usually calculate the hospital bill.

They rarely calculate:

Travel expenses.
Accommodation costs.
Caregiver support.
Lost workdays.
Additional medicines.
Follow-up consultations.
Emotional stress.

These invisible expenses often become a major burden.

Why Middle-Class Families Are Vulnerable

Middle-class families often have assets but limited liquidity.

Money is tied up in:

Homes.
Investments.
Retirement plans.
Children's education funds.
Business assets.

When emergencies occur, these assets become funding sources.

The family survives.

The financial plan suffers.

The Illusion of 'It Won't Happen to Me'

Most people believe serious illness happens to someone else.

Another family.
Another city.
Another neighborhood.

Until one day it happens to them.

A diagnosis does not check your calendar.

An emergency does not wait until your loans are repaid.

Illness follows its own timetable.

The Cost of Waiting

Many people postpone healthcare planning because they feel healthy today.

The most affordable time to prepare is before a crisis.

The most expensive time to prepare is during one.

Age	Premium Trend	Flexibility
30	Lowest	Highest
40	Moderate	Moderate
50	Higher	Limited

This principle applies to health insurance, emergency funds, critical illness protection, and preventive healthcare.

A Hard Truth

Most families are closer to financial vulnerability than they realize—not because they are irresponsible, but because they underestimate the financial power of a medical emergency.

Understanding this reality is not pessimism.

It is wisdom.

Part III

From Vulnerability to Protection

Why Smart People Ignore Healthcare Risk

One of the most fascinating aspects of human behavior is that intelligent people often ignore obvious risks.

They insure their vehicles.

They secure their homes.

They protect their smartphones.

Yet they often neglect the asset that makes everything else possible—their health.

Why?

Because illness feels distant.

Human beings are naturally optimistic. We believe bad things happen to other people.

Unfortunately, medical emergencies do not care about optimism.

The Financial Protection Pyramid

Over the years, I have developed a simple framework

called the Financial Protection Pyramid.

Level 1 – Emergency Fund

Every family should maintain immediate liquidity. Medical emergencies rarely arrive with notice.

Level 2 – Health Insurance

Insurance protects savings from large hospital bills.

Level 3 – Super Top-Up Protection

Healthcare inflation continues rising. Additional protection helps defend against catastrophic expenses.

Level 4 – Critical Illness Cover

Some illnesses affect income, business performance, and family goals long after hospitalization ends.

Level 5 – Wealth Creation

Only after protection is established should wealth creation become the primary focus.

Advisor's Corner

During my journey working with thousands of families, I noticed a simple pattern.
Families rarely regret buying protection.

They often regret delaying it.

I have met people who postponed insurance because they felt healthy.

I have met people who believed savings alone were sufficient.

I have met business owners who insured every asset except themselves.

Almost all of them wished they had acted earlier.

The Family Vulnerability Assessment

Answer the following questions honestly:

1. If a 1 ₹ 5 lakh. hospital bill arrived tomorrow, could you pay it comfortably?
2. Would you need to redeem investments?
3. Would your child's education fund remain untouched?
4. Could your family survive six months of reduced income?
5. Are your parents adequately protected?
6. Do you know where all policy documents are stored?

The answers reveal your current level of preparedness.

The Story Returns to Ramesh

Let us return to the hospital corridor where this chapter began.

Ramesh sat outside the ICU waiting for news about his father.

Hours passed.

Doctors worked tirelessly.

Family members prayed.

Eventually, good news arrived.

His father survived.

The relief was overwhelming.

But another challenge remained.

The bill.

The family managed.

Savings were used.
Investments were redeemed.
Financial goals were delayed.

Years later, Ramesh reflected on that experience.

The hospital bill did not destroy the family.

The lack of preparation almost did.

The Real Meaning of Wealth

Many people believe wealth means having money.

I believe wealth means having options.

The ability to make medical decisions without financial panic.

The ability to focus on recovery instead of bills.

The ability to protect your family's future while facing today's challenges.

That is true financial security.

Key Takeaways

- Medical emergencies create emotional and financial crises simultaneously.
- Healthcare costs extend beyond hospital bills.
- Income loss can be as damaging as treatment expenses.
- Protection and wealth creation must work together.
- Preparation is always cheaper than crisis management.
- Every family should build a Financial Protection Pyramid.

Final Thought

Imagine receiving a phone call at 2 a.m.

A loved one has been hospitalized.

In that moment, the difference between panic and confidence will not be your income.

It will be your preparation.

One hospital bill should never destroy a lifetime of dreams.

That is why this book exists.

That is why preparation matters.

And that is why the journey toward financial protection starts today.

Chapter 2

Why Healthcare Is Becoming the Biggest Financial Threat to Indian Families

Part I – The ₹18 lakh. Hospital Bill

It started with ordinary fatigue.

Rajiv, a 52-year-old manager from Pune, ignored his symptoms for weeks. One evening, he collapsed and was rushed to a private hospital. Within hours, he was admitted to the ICU.

The next morning, his family received an estimate.

₹18 lakh..

The number felt unreal.

Rajiv's family was not poor. They owned a flat, had investments, and maintained a respectable lifestyle. Yet a single medical emergency suddenly threatened years of financial planning.

This story is no longer unusual in India.

Across the country, families are discovering that healthcare costs have increased dramatically over the past decade. Treatments that once cost a few lakhs now often cost several times more because of advanced diagnostics, specialist care, robotic procedures, imported medical devices, and sophisticated ICU facilities.

Healthcare Inflation: The Silent Wealth Destroyer

Most families understand inflation when it comes to groceries, fuel, or school fees.

Few understand healthcare inflation.

Medical costs in India have consistently risen faster than general inflation. Industry reports over the years have regularly indicated healthcare inflation in high single digits or low double digits, meaning medical expenses can double far faster than many families expect.

Treatment	**Approx Cost**
Angioplasty	₹2– ₹ 5 lakh.
Bypass Surgery	₹3– ₹10 lakh.
Cancer Treatment	₹8–2 ₹ 5 lakh.+
ICU	₹20,000–₹50,000/day
Kidney Transplant	₹8–20 lakh+

Note -Costs vary by city, hospital, and complexity.

This creates a dangerous gap.

A family that believes ₹ 5 lakh. coverage is sufficient because it was adequate ten years ago may discover that the

same amount is no longer enough.
The New Reality of Healthcare Costs

Illustrative treatment costs often seen in private healthcare settings:

• Cardiac surgery: 3 lakh to ₹10 lakh. or more
• Cancer treatment: 8 lakh to 2 ₹ 5 lakh.+ depending on condition and duration
• Organ transplant procedures: Often significantly higher
• ICU stays: Tens of thousands of rupees per day
• Advanced diagnostics and follow-up care: Additional expenses that accumulate quickly

The purpose of these examples is not to create fear.

The purpose is to create awareness.

Many financial plans fail not because families are irresponsible, but because they underestimate the true cost of serious illness.

The Hidden Healthcare Crisis

Healthcare expenses rarely arrive alone.

When illness strikes, families face:

• Hospital bills
• Medicines
• Follow-up consultations

- Travel expenses
- Accommodation costs
- Loss of income
- Emotional stress

Most people prepare only for the hospital bill.

Very few prepare for everything else.

Part II
The Cost of Survival

Several years ago, I met a business owner who required major cardiac treatment.

The surgery was successful.

The hospital bill was substantial but manageable.

The larger problem appeared afterward.

For nearly six months, he was unable to operate his business at full capacity.

Revenue declined.

Customers shifted elsewhere.

Growth plans stopped.

The medical emergency affected not only his health but also his earning ability.

This is one of the most overlooked financial risks in India.

Illness affects both sides of the balance sheet:

Expenses increase.

Income may decrease.

The Education Fund That Disappeared

A young couple had spent nearly a decade building an education fund for their son.

Every month they invested systematically.

Then their child required emergency treatment.

The decision was easy.

The money was used.

The child recovered.

The education fund disappeared.

This story illustrates a simple truth:

Medical emergencies rarely pay for themselves.

They are often funded through:

- Savings
- Fixed deposits
- Mutual funds
- Retirement corpus
- Loans
- Borrowings from family and friends

The crisis ends.

The financial consequences remain.

Why Middle-Class Families Are Most Vulnerable

Many people assume only poor families struggle with healthcare costs.

In reality, middle-class families often face the greatest pressure.

Why?

Because they have something to lose.

They have:

- Homes
- Investments
- Retirement plans
- Education goals
- Business capital

A major health event can force difficult decisions regarding all of them.

The Illusion of "It Won't Happen to Me"

One of the most common financial planning mistakes is believing serious illness happens only to others.

Unfortunately:

Cancer does not check your age.

A heart attack does not wait for retirement.

A medical emergency does not care whether your financial planning is complete.

Healthcare risk exists whether we acknowledge it or not.

Part III – Preparing for a More Expensive Future

Most experts agree on one thing:

Healthcare will continue evolving.

New treatments will emerge.

Technology will improve.

Life expectancy may increase.

Unfortunately, costs are also likely to rise.

This means healthcare planning cannot be treated as a one-time decision.

It requires regular review.

A Family Healthcare Stress Test

Ask yourself:

1. Could your family comfortably handle a 15–20 lakh medical emergency?
2. Would you need to liquidate investments?
3. Would your child's education fund remain untouched?
4. Could your family survive six months of reduced income?
5. Are your parents adequately protected?
6. Do you review health insurance regularly?

These questions reveal financial resilience.

From My Experience

Throughout my years in banking, life insurance, health insurance, and financial services, I have noticed a consistent pattern.

Families rarely regret preparing early.

They often regret waiting.

The strongest families are not always the wealthiest.

They are usually the most prepared.

They understand healthcare risk.

They maintain protection.

They review their plans.

They take action before a crisis arrives.

Closing Story

Several years after Rajiv's hospitalization, his family looked back at the experience differently.

They were grateful he survived.

But they also realized something important.

The hospitalization exposed weaknesses in their financial planning.

Those weaknesses were corrected.

Coverage was increased.

Emergency reserves were strengthened.

Healthcare planning became a priority.

Their story reflects the central message of this chapter.

Healthcare is becoming one of the biggest financial threats facing Indian families.

The goal is not fear.

The goal is preparation.

Families cannot control every diagnosis.

But they can control how prepared they are when life becomes unpredictable.

And that preparation often determines whether a medical emergency becomes a temporary setback—or a long-term financial disaster.

Chapter 3

Health Insurance Made Simple: The Financial Shield Every Family Needs

Introduction

At 9:20 on a Monday morning, Rohit's phone rang.

The caller was a hospital administrator.

His father had been admitted following a cardiac emergency.

Before Rohit could fully understand the medical situation, another question arrived.

"Can you arrange an initial deposit of 2 lakh?"

Like many middle-class families, Rohit believed he was financially prepared. He had savings, investments, and a stable job. Yet that single phone call revealed something important.

There is a difference between having money and having protection.

That difference is called health insurance.

The 6 Lakh Phone Call

A few years ago, a salaried employee named Sanjay received a call that changed his understanding of financial planning forever.

His wife required emergency surgery.

The treatment was successful, but the total hospital bill crossed 6 lakh.

Fortunately, Sanjay had purchased health insurance several years earlier.

The claim was approved.

The family's savings remained intact.

After discharge, Sanjay said something powerful:

"I thought insurance was an expense. That day I realized it was protection."

Why Health Insurance Matters

Most people buy insurance hoping they never need it.

Nobody wants hospitalization.

Nobody plans for surgery.

Nobody schedules a medical emergency.

Yet healthcare costs continue rising.

Modern medicine saves lives, but advanced treatment often comes with significant expense.

Health insurance exists because families should not have to choose between medical treatment and financial stability.

A teacher from Pune.

Health insurance cover: ₹10 lakh..

Cancer treatment: 8. ₹ 5 lakh..

Insurance paid.

Education fund remained untouched.

Two Friends, Two Decisions

Consider the story of Amit and Rohit.

Both were thirty years old.

Both had similar incomes.

Both were healthy.

Amit purchased health insurance immediately.

Rohit postponed the decision.

He believed he could buy it later.

Fifteen years passed.

Amit's policy continued uninterrupted.

His coverage increased over time.

Waiting periods were completed.

Benefits accumulated.

Rohit finally decided to buy insurance at age forty-five.

The premium was higher.

Medical underwriting was stricter.

Certain conditions required additional evaluation.

The difference was not intelligence.

The difference was timing.

One of the most important lessons in insurance is simple:

The best time to buy health insurance is before you need it.

Many people avoid insurance because they believe it is complicated.

In reality, the core concepts are straightforward.

Sum Insured

The sum insured is the maximum coverage available under the policy during a policy year.

Imagine carrying an umbrella during a storm.

A larger umbrella generally provides greater protection.

Similarly, adequate coverage helps protect against larger medical expenses.

Cashless Claims

Cashless treatment allows eligible expenses to be settled directly between the insurer and the hospital according to policy terms.

For families facing a medical emergency, this can reduce immediate financial pressure.

Reimbursement Claims

Sometimes treatment occurs at a hospital where cashless service is unavailable.

In such situations, families pay expenses initially and later submit documents for reimbursement according to policy conditions.

Network Hospitals

Insurance companies maintain networks of hospitals where cashless treatment may be available.

Understanding nearby network hospitals before an emergency occurs can be extremely valuable.

Waiting Periods

Many policies include waiting periods for specific conditions or benefits.

This is another reason why delaying insurance purchases can be costly.

No Claim Bonus

Some policies reward claim-free years by increasing available coverage or providing other benefits.

Over time, these features can significantly improve protection.

The Four Biggest Myths

Myth 1: I Am Healthy

Most people who purchase health insurance are healthy when they buy it.

That is exactly the point.

Insurance becomes easier to obtain before medical conditions develop.

Myth 2: My Employer Covers Me

Employer coverage is valuable, but it may not always be sufficient.

Job changes, retirement, and coverage limitations create risks.

Personal coverage provides additional security.

Myth 3: Insurance Is Expensive

Many families underestimate healthcare costs while overestimating insurance costs.

One hospitalization may cost far more than years of premiums.

Myth 4: Claims Never Get Paid

Successful claims occur every day.

Most claim difficulties arise from misunderstandings,

documentation issues, or non-disclosure rather than the concept of insurance itself.

Lessons From Real Families

During my years at Star Health, I met a family from Pune who delayed buying health insurance because they believed serious illness would never affect them.

I have also met families who purchased coverage early and later protected their savings during difficult times.

One family used insurance during a major hospitalization and preserved the education fund they had built for their daughter.

Another family relied entirely on savings because they believed insurance was unnecessary.

The financial outcomes were dramatically different.

The Role of Health Insurance in Wealth Creation

Many people think of insurance and investments as separate topics.

In reality, they work together.

Investments help create wealth.

Insurance helps protect wealth.

Without protection, years of disciplined investing can be disrupted by a single medical event.

The strongest financial plans balance both.

Health Insurance Readiness Checklist

Ask yourself:

Do I have personal health insurance?

Is my coverage adequate for today's healthcare costs?

Do I know my nearest network hospital?

Have I reviewed my policy during the past year?

Do family members know where policy documents are stored?

Are my parents adequately protected?

Every unanswered question represents an opportunity to strengthen protection.

Advisor's Corner

Throughout my career in banking, life insurance, health insurance, and financial services, I have observed one consistent pattern.

Families rarely regret buying health insurance.

They often regret postponing the decision.

Most people think health insurance is about hospital bills.

It is actually about protecting goals.

Retirement goals.

Education goals.

Business goals.

Family goals.

The policy protects much more than medical expenses.

It protects the future.

Final Story

Several years after his father's hospitalization, Rohit looked back on the experiencc differently.

The hospital bill had been substantial.

The emotional stress had been intense.

Yet one lesson remained clear.

Preparation creates options.

Because protection existed, the family focused on recovery

instead of fundraising.

They focused on treatment instead of financial panic.

That is the true purpose of health insurance.

Conclusion

Health insurance is not a financial product purchased out of fear.

A father standing outside ICU.

The doctor said, "Treatment can start immediately."

He doesn't ask:"How much money do I have?"

Because protection already exists.

It is a protection tool purchased out of responsibility.

The objective is simple.

When a medical emergency occurs, families should be able to focus on health rather than financial survival.

The families who understand this lesson early gain something valuable.

Confidence.
And in times of crisis, confidence is priceless.

Chapter 4

How Much Health Insurance Do You Really Need? The Costly Mistake Most Families Make

Introduction

In 2012, the Kulkarni family purchased a health insurance policy with a sum insured of ₹ 5 lakh..

At that time, the coverage felt more than adequate.

The family felt protected.

They believed they had done the right thing.

For years, the policy was renewed without much thought.

Then in 2026, everything changed.

A cancer diagnosis resulted in hospitalization, surgery, medicines, and follow-up treatment.

The total medical expense crossed ₹ ₹18 lakh..

The insurance policy paid ₹ 5 lakh..

The remaining 13 lakh had to come from savings, investments, and borrowed money.

The problem was not that the family lacked insurance.

The problem was that they had too little insurance.

This chapter is about avoiding that costly mistake.

Why Most Families Are Underinsured

Many families purchase health insurance based on affordability rather than actual need.

When an insurance advisor asks about coverage, people often ask:

"What is the cheapest option available?"

A better question is:

"What amount of protection would my family actually need during a serious medical emergency?"

Healthcare costs have changed dramatically over the last decade.

Advanced technology, specialist doctors, expensive medicines, and rising medical inflation have increased treatment costs significantly.

A cover amount that seemed sufficient ten years ago may no longer provide adequate protection today.

The Real Cost of Modern Healthcare

Consider some common medical situations.

A major cardiac procedure can cost several lakhs.

Cancer treatment may continue for months and sometimes years.

An ICU admission can generate substantial expenses within a short period.

The challenge is not only the cost.

The challenge is uncertainty.

No family knows exactly when illness will occur or how much treatment may eventually cost.

That uncertainty makes adequate coverage essential.

The Three Coverage Mistakes

Mistake Number One – Buying the Minimum Cover

Many people purchase the smallest policy available because they focus on premium rather than protection.

The premium may be lower.

The risk remains higher.

Insurance should be viewed as protection, not merely a purchase.

Mistake Number Two – Ignoring Parents

Many families focus only on themselves and their children.

Parents often remain underinsured.

As healthcare needs increase with age, this can create significant financial pressure.

Mistake Number Three – Never Reviewing Coverage

Healthcare costs rise.

Family circumstances change.

Income grows.

Responsibilities increase.

Yet many policies remain unchanged for years.

Protection should evolve alongside life.

Three Families, Three Outcomes

Family A

Coverage: ₹ 5 lakh.

Medical Event: Cancer treatment costing 1 ₹ 5 lakh.

Result:

Insurance helped, but a substantial financial gap remained.

Family B

Coverage: 1 ₹ 5 lakh.

Medical Event: Similar treatment cost

Result:

Most expenses were covered.

Financial stress reduced significantly.

Family C

Coverage: 2 ₹ 5 lakh. plus Super Top-Up

Medical Event: Similar treatment cost

Result:

Treatment proceeded without major disruption to long-term financial goals.

The lesson is simple.

The same illness can create completely different financial outcomes depending on preparation.

A Simple Family Coverage Framework

Family Example:

Husband – Age 38

Wife – Age 35

Two Children

Urban Location

Suggested Approach:

Adequate base health insurance.

Additional super top-up coverage.

Annual review process.

Emergency fund support.

The objective is not predicting every medical event.

The objective is creating financial resilience.

From My Experience

Throughout my years working in banking, life insurance, health insurance, and financial services, I have met families across every income category.

One common pattern appears repeatedly.

Families rarely regret having too much protection.

They often regret having too little.

Many people discover coverage gaps only after hospitalization.

By then, options are limited.

The best time to review protection is before a crisis occurs.

The Family Protection Worksheet

Ask yourself:

How much health insurance does my family currently have?

When was the last review conducted?

Would my current coverage handle a 20 lakh hospitalization?

Are my parents adequately protected?

Do I have additional super top-up coverage?

Could my savings remain intact during a major medical event?

These questions help identify vulnerabilities.

The Cost of Waiting

Some people delay increasing coverage because they feel healthy.

Others postpone reviews because life becomes busy.

Unfortunately, healthcare risks do not wait.

A diagnosis does not check your calendar.

An emergency does not ask whether your financial planning is complete.

Preparation must happen before the crisis.

Final Story

A father once told me something I never forgot.

Standing outside an ICU, he realized his family had insurance.

But he also realized it was not enough.

The issue was not the policy.

The issue was the amount of protection.

That experience changed how he viewed financial planning.

Years later he increased coverage, added additional protection, and reviewed his family's plan regularly.

His advice to others was simple:

"Do not ask how much insurance you can afford.

Ask how much protection your family may need."

Conclusion

The goal of health insurance is not merely owning a policy.

The goal is ensuring that when a serious medical emergency occurs, the family can focus on treatment rather than financial survival.

Adequate coverage creates confidence.

Adequate coverage protects goals.

Adequate coverage protects the future.

And that protection may become one of the most valuable financial decisions a family ever makes.

Chapter 5

The Fine Print That Saves (or Sinks) You

Introduction

Most people spend days comparing premiums but only a few minutes reviewing the policy document.

That is one of the biggest mistakes in health insurance.

When families buy a policy, they often focus on the coverage amount, premium, and brand name. Very few pay attention to the clauses hidden inside the policy wording.

Unfortunately, during a claim, those clauses become more important than the marketing brochure.

The difference between a successful claim and an unpleasant surprise often lies in the fine print.

The Story of Rajesh

Rajesh was a successful IT professional from Pune.

After comparing several health insurance plans, he selected a policy offering a ₹10 lakh. sum insured.

He felt confident about his decision.

Years later, his wife required hospitalization.

Since they wanted the best comfort available, Rajesh selected a premium room.

At discharge, he was shocked.

A portion of the bill was not fully payable under the policy.

The reason was simple.

His policy contained a room rent limitation.

Rajesh had health insurance.

What he lacked was understanding.

That experience taught him a lesson he never forgot:

Buying insurance is easy.

Understanding insurance is valuable.

Why the Fine Print Matters

Imagine purchasing a house without reading the ownership documents.

Imagine investing in a business without reviewing the agreement.

Most people would never do that.

Yet many buy health insurance without reading the policy wording.

The fine print exists to explain exactly how the policy works.

It defines:

What is covered.

What is excluded.

When coverage begins.

How claims are evaluated.

What limitations apply.

The policy document is the real contract.

Everything else is merely a summary.

Case Study: The Hernia Surprise

Mr. Sharma purchased health insurance and assumed every medical condition would be covered immediately.

Six months later, he required hernia surgery.

The claim was not approved because the policy contained a waiting period for specific conditions.

Mr. Sharma was frustrated.

The insurer pointed to the policy wording.

The lesson was not that the insurer was wrong.

The lesson was that the customer never understood the waiting period.

Understanding Waiting Periods

Waiting periods are among the most misunderstood features in health insurance.

A waiting period is the duration during which specific benefits may not be available.

Common examples include:

Initial waiting periods.

Disease-specific waiting periods.

Pre-existing disease waiting periods.

Waiting periods encourage long-term planning and prevent misuse of insurance.

This is why buying health insurance early creates a major advantage.

Time works in your favor.

The Cost of Delaying Insurance

Consider two individuals.

Amit buys insurance at age thirty.

Rohit waits until age forty-five.

When health conditions appear later in life, Amit has already completed waiting periods.

Rohit is just beginning them.

The difference is not luck.

The difference is preparation.

The Hidden Danger of Non-Disclosure

During my years in health insurance, I repeatedly noticed one mistake.

People hide information.

Sometimes they fear higher premiums.

Sometimes they believe the condition is minor.

Sometimes they simply forget.

Regardless of the reason, non-disclosure creates risk.

Case Study: The Diabetes Claim

A businessman purchased health insurance at age forty-eight.

He had already been diagnosed with diabetes but chose not to disclose it.

Several years later, he required hospitalization.

Medical records revealed the earlier diagnosis.

The claim investigation became complicated.

The problem was not diabetes.

The problem was incomplete disclosure.

Insurance works best when information is accurate and complete.

Understanding Exclusions

Every policy contains exclusions.

These are situations where coverage may not apply.

Examples may include:

Cosmetic procedures.

Experimental treatments.

Certain non-medical expenses.

Policy-defined exclusions.

Exclusions are not hidden traps.

They define the boundaries of coverage.

A good buyer understands those boundaries before purchasing.

The Room Rent Trap

Room rent clauses have surprised many policyholders.

A room rent restriction may appear insignificant during purchase.

During hospitalization, however, it can affect multiple bill components.

Because many hospital charges are linked to room category, selecting a room beyond policy limits may increase out-of-pocket expenses.

This is why understanding room eligibility is important.

The Co-Payment Story

Mrs. Patel purchased a policy because the premium was lower than other options.

Years later she required treatment costing ₹ 5 lakh..

Only then did she discover that her policy contained a co-payment clause.

She had to contribute part of the expense herself.

The policy worked exactly as designed.

The issue was that she never understood the clause.

A lower premium sometimes comes with additional conditions.

The Importance of Network Hospitals

Cashless treatment is one of the most valuable features of health insurance.

However, it depends heavily on network hospitals.

Imagine a medical emergency occurring at midnight.

The last thing a family wants is uncertainty about claim procedures.

Before purchasing a policy, always review:

Nearby hospitals.

Emergency care facilities.

Preferred specialists.

Network availability.

Preparation before hospitalization reduces stress during hospitalization.

The Cataract Lesson

Mrs. Shah had a policy with a substantial sum insured.

Years later she underwent cataract surgery.

To her surprise, the claim payout was limited.

The reason was a treatment-specific sub-limit.

The overall coverage amount was large.

The cataract limit was smaller.

This experience highlights an important truth:

Coverage amount alone does not tell the entire story.

The Claims Perspective

Most claim disputes arise from misunderstandings.

Customers assume coverage exists.

Insurers refer to policy wording.

The gap between expectation and reality creates frustration.

Policy understanding reduces this gap.

Knowledge before hospitalization prevents disappointment afterward.

The Fine Print Review Checklist

Before purchasing any policy, review:

Waiting periods.

Room rent conditions.

Co-payments.

Sub-limits.

Exclusions.

Network hospitals.

Restoration benefits.

Claim procedures.

Renewability conditions.

A one-hour review can save significant financial stress later.

From My Experience

During my years in banking, life insurance, and health insurance, I have observed a consistent pattern.

Families rarely regret reading policy documents.

They frequently regret ignoring them.

The most confident policyholders are not insurance experts.

They simply understand the important clauses affecting their protection.

Knowledge creates confidence.

Confidence improves decision-making.

Reality Check Exercise

Take out your current health insurance policy and answer:

What is the waiting period?

Does the policy contain co-payments?

Are there room rent restrictions?

What are the major exclusions?

Which hospitals provide cashless treatment?

Can you explain the claim process?

If you cannot answer these questions confidently, your policy deserves a detailed review.

Common Mistakes

Buying insurance only because it is cheap.

Ignoring policy wording.

Depending entirely on verbal promises.

Failing to disclose medical history.

Never reviewing policy documents.

Assuming all policies are identical.

Avoiding these mistakes dramatically improves claim experience.

Key Takeaways

The fine print matters.

Waiting periods influence eligibility.

Room rent conditions affect claims.

Co-payments increase out-of-pocket costs.

Sub-limits may restrict payouts.

Exclusions define coverage boundaries.

Understanding improves outcomes.

Final Story

A father once told me:

"When I bought health insurance, I thought the policy document was the least important part.

When I made a claim, I realized it was the most important part."

That statement perfectly summarizes this chapter.

Conclusion

Health insurance is not merely about buying a policy.

It is about understanding what you have purchased.

The families who benefit most from health insurance are not necessarily those who buy the most expensive plans.

They are the families who understand their protection.

A few hours spent reviewing the fine print today can save enormous stress tomorrow.

The fine print may appear boring.

But during a medical emergency, it often becomes the most valuable part of the policy.

Chapter 6

Family Floater vs Individual Plans (And What to Do for Parents)

Introduction

One of the most confusing decisions in health insurance is choosing between a Family Floater Policy and Individual Health Insurance Plans.

Many families purchase a policy without understanding the long-term impact of this decision. Initially, everything appears fine because there are no claims. Years later, when a major hospitalization occurs, they discover that the structure of the policy matters just as much as the coverage amount.

The objective of health insurance is not simply to buy a policy. The objective is to create a protection structure that works for every member of the family.

This chapter will help you understand the advantages, disadvantages, and ideal use cases for both Family Floater and Individual Plans so that you can make an informed decision.

Understanding Family Floater Plans

A Family Floater Plan provides a single sum insured that is shared among all covered family members.

For example, if a family purchases a 20 lakh family floater policy covering husband, wife, and two children, the entire family shares the 20 lakh coverage.

The advantage is simplicity.

One policy.

One renewal date.

One premium.

Shared protection.

This structure works especially well when family members are young and healthy.

Why Family Floater Plans Became Popular

Insurance companies introduced family floater plans because most families do not experience multiple major hospitalizations simultaneously.

A shared pool of coverage often provides efficient protection at a lower cost than purchasing separate policies for every family member.

For young families, this can be a practical solution.

A husband may never claim.

The children may remain healthy.

The wife may require only routine healthcare.

In such situations, the entire coverage remains available

whenever needed.

The Biggest Advantage of Family Floaters

Cost efficiency.

This is the primary reason many families choose family floater plans.

A single 20 lakh floater often costs less than buying four separate individual policies with the same aggregate protection.

For young families, the premium savings can be substantial.

The Hidden Risk of Family Floaters

Every benefit has a trade-off.

The biggest risk is coverage sharing.

Imagine a family with 20 lakh floater coverage.

One member undergoes a complicated treatment costing 1 ₹ 5 lakh..

Only ₹ 5 lakh. remains available for the rest of the family during that policy year.

This may not create a problem most years.

However, if multiple hospitalizations occur, the limitation becomes obvious.

Case Study: The Kulkarni Family

Mr. Kulkarni purchased a 1 ₹ 5 lakh. family floater covering himself, his wife, and two children.

The arrangement worked perfectly for several years.

Then his wife required a major surgery costing 11 lakh.

A few months later, one child required hospitalization after an accident.

Although the policy helped significantly, the remaining coverage was limited.

The family realized that a large claim by one member affects everyone covered under the floater.

Understanding Individual Health Insurancc Plans

Individual policies operate differently.

Each family member receives a separate sum insurcd.

If a husband has ₹10 lakh. coverage and the wife has ₹10 lakh. coverage, their limits remain independent.

One person's claim does not reduce another person's protection.

This structure provides greater certainty but generally costs more.

The Benefits of Individual Plans

The biggest advantage is dedicated coverage.

Each insured person has protection reserved exclusively for them.

Even if one family member exhausts their policy, others remain unaffected.

This creates stronger protection for families with higher health risks.

When Individual Plans Make Sense

Individual plans are often suitable for:

People with chronic illnesses.

Families with older members.

Individuals requiring specialized protection.

People who want complete separation of coverage.

The premium may be higher, but the protection is also more personalized.

What About Children?

Young children usually have lower hospitalization frequency compared to older adults.

For many families, including children in a family floater plan is practical and economical.

However, as children grow older and become financially independent, separate policies may become appropriate.

The Parent Protection Challenge

One of the most important health insurance decisions involves parents.

Many people assume they should simply add parents to a family floater policy.

This is not always the best strategy.

Parents generally have:

Higher hospitalization probability.

Age-related health conditions.

Greater healthcare utilization.

More frequent medical consultations.

Adding elderly parents to a floater can significantly increase premiums.

Why Parents Often Need Separate Policies

Separate senior citizen plans offer advantages.

Coverage can be tailored specifically to their age group.

Benefits may be designed around common senior health needs.

Most importantly, their claims do not affect coverage available for younger family members.

Case Study: Two Different Approaches

Family A included parents in a large family floater policy.

Family B maintained separate coverage for parents and a separate floater for the core family.

When the father required hospitalization, Family B experienced far less disruption because the claim affected only the parent's policy.

This illustrates why policy structure matters.

The Hybrid Strategy

In many cases, the most effective solution is a hybrid approach.

Core Family:

Family Floater.

Father uses 12 lakh.

Mother hospitalized later.

Floater almost exhausted.

Parents:

Separate Individual Policies.

This structure combines affordability and protection.

Many experienced advisors recommend this arrangement because it balances cost and risk effectively.

The Role of Super Top-Up Plans

Super top-up plans can strengthen both structures.

Whether using a family floater or individual plans, a super top-up can provide additional protection against large medical expenses.

This creates an extra safety layer without dramatically increasing premiums.

Advisor Insight

Throughout my insurance career, I have noticed that people often focus entirely on premium.

The better question is:

How will this structure perform during a claim?

A policy should not only look attractive during purchase.

It should function effectively during a medical emergency.

The best insurance decisions are made by imagining future claim scenarios rather than current premium amounts.

Questions Every Family Should Ask

How many members require coverage?

What are their ages?

Do parents require protection?

Are there existing health conditions?

What is the family budget?

How much coverage is needed?

The answers help determine the ideal structure.

Common Mistakes

Adding elderly parents to a floater without understanding premium impact.

Choosing the cheapest option.

Ignoring claim-sharing risk.

Never reviewing coverage as family circumstances change.

Depending solely on employer insurance.

Avoiding these mistakes improves long-term protection.

Reality Check Exercise

Review your current arrangement.

Is coverage shared or individual?

How would a large claim affect the remaining family members?

Are parents adequately protected?

Would current coverage remain sufficient if healthcare costs doubled?

The answers may reveal opportunities for improvement.

Key Takeaways

Family floaters provide shared coverage and cost efficiency.

Individual plans provide dedicated protection.

Parents often require separate consideration.

Policy structure matters as much as policy amount.

Hybrid strategies frequently provide the best balance.

Coverage should evolve with family needs.

Conclusion

There is no universally perfect answer when choosing between Family Floater and Individual Health Insurancc Plans.

The correct choice depends on age, health profile, family size, parents' needs, financial goals, and risk tolerance.

The objective is not simply to buy insurance.

The objective is to create a protection structure capable of supporting the entire family during difficult times.

When chosen correctly, health insurance becomes more than a policy.

It becomes a foundation of financial stability and peace of mind.

In the next chapter, we will uncover the truth about Employer Health Insurance and why depending entirely on workplace coverage may be one of the biggest mistakes professionals make.

Chapter 7

The Truth About Employer Health Insurance: Why Your Company Policy Is Not Enough

Introduction

When Rahul joined a leading multinational company in Pune, he felt financially secure.

The company offered an attractive salary package, performance incentives, retirement benefits, and a health insurance policy covering his entire family.

For years, Rahul proudly told friends:

"I already have health insurance. My company takes care of it."

Like millions of professionals across India, he believed employer-provided health insurance was enough.

Then life changed.

During the COVID period, his company restructured operations. Rahul lost his job.

At first, his concern was income.

A few months later, a second concern appeared.

His father required hospitalization.

That was the day Rahul discovered an important truth:

His health insurance belonged to the company—not to him.

The Comfort of Corporate Coverage

Employer health insurance is one of the most valuable benefits offered by organizations.

It provides immediate protection.

Employees do not have to undergo extensive medical underwriting.

Premiums are usually paid fully or partially by the employer.

Coverage often extends to spouses and children.

For young professionals, it creates a sense of financial safety.

And to be fair, employer coverage is extremely useful.

The problem begins when people mistake convenience for complete protection.

The Biggest Question Most Employees Never Ask

Ask a salaried professional:

"Do you have health insurance?"

The answer is usually yes.

Ask another question:

"If you resign tomorrow, what happens to your family's health insurance?"

Most people have never seriously considered the answer.

This is where the real risk exists.

The danger is not lack of insurance.

The danger is dependence on insurance controlled by someone else.

The COVID Lesson

The pandemic taught India many lessons.

One of those lessons involved healthcare protection.

Thousands of employees changed jobs.

Many lost employment.

Some started businesses.

Others accepted salary cuts or moved to different industries.

During that period, many families realized that employer insurance could disappear unexpectedly.

For years they believed they were protected.

Then they discovered they had no independent healthcare safety net.

The Story of Vikas

Vikas worked for a multinational company for more than twelve years.

His employer provided excellent health insurance coverage.

Because of this, he never purchased a personal policy.

At age forty-five, he decided to leave his job and start a consulting business.

Only then did he begin exploring personal health insurance.

The timing was unfortunate.

Over the years he had developed hypertension and diabetes.

Premiums were higher.

Medical disclosures became more complicated.

Some options were no longer available.

Looking back, he admitted:

"I should have bought personal insurance while I was healthy and employed."

Employer Insurance Has Advantages

This chapter is not intended to criticize employer insurance.

Corporate health insurance provides several important benefits:

Immediate coverage.

Cashless hospitalization.

Group pricing advantages.

Coverage for family members.

Reduced financial burden.

Access to network hospitals.

Many employees experience their first health insurance

protection through employer-sponsored plans.

These benefits are real and valuable.

The problem arises only when people stop there.

The Retirement Problem

Consider a simple question.

At what stage of life do healthcare expenses usually increase?

The answer is obvious.

Retirement years.

As people grow older, healthcare needs generally increase.

Doctor visits become more frequent.

Lifestyle diseases become more common.

Hospitalization risk increases.

Ironically, this is exactly when employer health insurance typically disappears.

Many retirees suddenly discover they no longer have the protection they depended upon for decades.

The Cost of Waiting

Health insurance becomes more expensive with age.

This is true across most insurance products.

A person buying insurance at age thirty generally has more options than someone buying it at fifty-five.

Buying early provides advantages:

Lower premiums.

Completed waiting periods.

Better continuity.

Greater flexibility.

Future insurability.

The earlier protection begins, the stronger the long-term foundation becomes.

Case Study: Two Different Professionals

Amit and Kunal joined their companies at almost the same age.

Both received employer health insurance.

Amit purchased a personal policy in addition to employer coverage.

Kunal relied entirely on corporate insurance.

Fifteen years later, both left their jobs.

Amit's personal policy continued seamlessly.

His waiting periods were completed.

His protection remained intact.

Kunal had to start from scratch.

The difference was not income.

The difference was planning.

Employer Insurance Is Controlled by the Employer

This is one of the most overlooked realities.

When you own a personal policy, you control the coverage.

When you rely entirely on employer insurance, many important decisions are made elsewhere.

Coverage limits can change.

Insurers can change.

Benefits can change.

Conditions can change.

The employer has every right to modify the plan.

The employee has limited influence.

This creates uncertainty.

Healthcare Inflation Changes Everything

Healthcare costs continue increasing.

A coverage amount that looked impressive ten years ago may feel inadequate today.

A major hospitalization involving cancer, cardiac treatment, organ transplant procedures, or prolonged ICU stays can generate expenses that exceed expectations.

Corporate coverage may help significantly.

But depending entirely on one layer of protection can create risk.

Why Personal Insurance Creates Freedom

One of the greatest benefits of personal insurance is flexibility.

Career decisions become easier.

Entrepreneurship becomes easier.

Retirement planning becomes easier.

Job changes become easier.

Because healthcare protection remains intact, families can make life decisions without worrying about losing insurance.

Insurance creates freedom.

Dependence creates limitations.

The Family Perspective

Healthcare planning should never be viewed only from the employee's perspective.

It must be viewed from the family's perspective.

Spouses depend on continuity.

Children depend on stability.

Parents depend on preparation.

When healthcare protection is tied entirely to employment,

the family becomes vulnerable to employment changes.

Independent insurance creates continuity.

The Layered Protection Strategy

Over the years, I have found that the strongest families often use a layered approach.

Layer One:
Employer Coverage

Layer Two:
Personal Health Insurance

Layer Three:
Super Top-Up Protection

Each layer strengthens the next.

If one layer changes, the others continue providing support.

This creates resilience.

The Business Transition Story

A successful sales manager decided to become an entrepreneur.

The opportunity looked promising.

Business plans were ready.

Funding was arranged.

Yet one issue almost delayed the entire project.

Healthcare protection.

His family's insurance existed only through his employer.

Before resigning, he purchased independent coverage and created a long-term protection plan.

This decision gave him confidence.

He was no longer dependent on corporate benefits.

His protection moved with him.

That is how insurance should work.

From My Experience

Throughout my years in banking, life insurance, health insurance, and financial services, I have met many professionals who believed employer insurance was sufficient.

Most of them realized the limitation only when circumstances changed.

Some changed jobs.

Some retired.

Some became self-employed.

Others faced health conditions that made later insurance purchases more complicated.

The professionals who maintained independent coverage experienced far less stress.

Their planning created flexibility.

Their protection created confidence.

Reality Check Exercise

Ask yourself:

If I resign tomorrow, does my family remain protected?

Do I know my employer policy coverage amount?

Do I know its exclusions?

Do I have a personal backup plan?

Have I reviewed my family's healthcare needs recently?

Would retirement affect my healthcare security?

Your answers reveal the strength of your protection strategy.

Common Mistakes

Depending entirely on employer insurance.

Ignoring retirement healthcare planning.

Postponing personal coverage.

Assuming corporate benefits will never change.

Never reviewing policy details.

Believing health insurance can be purchased easily later.

Avoiding these mistakes improves long-term financial security.

Key Takeaways

Employer health insurance is valuable but temporary.

Coverage is linked to employment.

Retirement can create protection gaps.

Job changes can affect healthcare security.

Personal insurance creates continuity.

The strongest strategy combines employer and personal protection.

Conclusion

Employer health insurance is an excellent benefit.

It provides meaningful protection and financial support during employment.

But it should never be the only healthcare strategy a family relies upon.

Jobs change.

Companies change.

Industries change.

Life changes.

Healthcare needs continue.

The goal is not merely to have health insurance today.

The goal is to ensure your family remains protected tomorrow, next year, and decades from now.

Health insurance should belong to your family—not to your employer.

Chapter 8

Pre-Existing Diseases, Waiting Periods and Underwriting

Introduction

One of the biggest reasons people postpone buying health insurance is the belief that they will purchase it later when they need it. Unfortunately, health insurance does not work that way.

The best time to buy health insurance is when you are healthy. The second-best time is today.

The moment a medical condition develops, health insurance becomes more complicated. Premiums may increase, waiting periods become important, underwriting becomes stricter, and policy choices may become limited.

This chapter explains three concepts that every policyholder must understand: Pre-Existing Diseases, Waiting Periods, and Underwriting.

These three factors often determine whether a policy becomes a powerful financial shield or a source of disappointment.

What Is a Pre-Existing Disease?

A pre-existing disease is generally a medical condition,

illness, injury, or symptom that existed before purchasing a health insurance policy.

Common examples include:

Diabetes

Hypertension

Asthma

Thyroid disorders

Heart disease

Kidney disorders

Arthritis

The exact definition varies by insurer and policy wording, but the principle remains the same.

If a health condition exists before policy purchase, insurers want to understand that risk before offering coverage.

Why Insurers Care About Pre-Existing Diseases

Many customers feel uncomfortable when insurers ask detailed medical questions.

However, insurance companies are not trying to reject customers.

They are trying to evaluate risk accurately.

Imagine someone purchases fire insurance after their house

catches fire.

The insurer would obviously face a problem.

Similarly, health insurance is designed to protect against future uncertainty—not known and immediate expenses.

This is why disclosure is so important.

The Most Common Mistake: Hiding Medical History

Throughout the insurance industry, one mistake appears repeatedly.

People hide medical information.

Some fear policy rejection.

Others worry about premium increases.

A few believe a minor health issue is not important enough to mention.

Unfortunately, this decision can create major claim complications later.

Insurance works best when everything is disclosed honestly from the beginning.

Case Study: The Hidden Diabetes Problem

Mr. Shah purchased a health insurance policy at age 48.

He had been diagnosed with diabetes two years earlier but decided not to disclose it because he feared higher premiums.

Several years later he required hospitalization related to diabetes complications.

During claim evaluation, medical records revealed the earlier diagnosis.

The claim process became difficult and stressful.

The issue was not diabetes.

The issue was non-disclosure.

Honesty at purchase often prevents disputes later.

Understanding Waiting Periods

Waiting periods are among the most misunderstood aspects of health insurance.

Many people believe that once the policy starts, every illness is immediately covered.

This assumption is often incorrect.

Most policies contain waiting periods.

A waiting period is simply a specific duration during which certain benefits are restricted or unavailable.

Why Waiting Periods Exist

Insurance companies use waiting periods to prevent misuse.

Without waiting periods, individuals could wait until they needed treatment and then immediately buy insurance.

This would make the insurance system unsustainable.

Waiting periods help create fairness for all policyholders.

Types of Waiting Periods

Initial Waiting Period

Most policies contain an initial waiting period after policy issuance.

Certain situations, such as accidents, may be treated differently according to policy conditions.

Specific Disease Waiting Period

Some medical conditions have separate waiting periods.

Examples may include:

Hernia

Cataract

Joint replacement procedures

Certain surgeries

Pre-Existing Disease Waiting Period

Pre-existing diseases often have their own waiting period before related claims become eligible.

This is one reason buying health insurance early is so valuable.

The waiting period starts immediately after policy purchase.

The sooner coverage begins, the sooner waiting periods are completed.

Case Study: Early Planning Pays Off

Amit purchased health insurance at age 32.

At age 37 he developed hypertension.

Because his policy had been active for years, waiting periods had already been completed.

When hospitalization became necessary later, he benefited from continuous coverage.

The decision to buy early created a significant advantage.

What Is Underwriting?

Underwriting is the process insurers use to evaluate risk.

Many policyholders never hear this term until they apply for coverage.

However, underwriting plays a critical role.

During underwriting, insurers assess factors such as:

Age

Medical history

Lifestyle habits

Occupation

Existing illnesses

Previous surgeries

Family medical history

The goal is to understand risk before issuing coverage.

Why Two People Receive Different Outcomes

Consider two individuals.

Both are 45 years old.

Both apply for the same health insurance policy.

One exercises regularly, has no medical history, and maintains a healthy lifestyle.

The second has diabetes, hypertension, and a history of hospitalization.

Even though they are the same age, their risk profiles differ significantly.

Underwriting helps insurers evaluate those differences.

Possible Underwriting Decisions

After evaluation, an insurer may:

Issue the policy as requested.

Request additional medical tests.

Offer modified terms.

Apply exclusions according to policy rules.

Request further information.

Every case is unique.

The Role of Medical Tests

Many applicants become nervous when insurers request medical examinations.

In reality, medical tests often benefit both parties.

They help insurers assess risk accurately.

They also help applicants understand their current health status.

Common tests may include:

Blood sugar evaluation

Blood pressure assessment

Cardiac screening

Liver function tests

Kidney function tests

Urine analysis

The exact requirements vary based on age, health profile, and insurer guidelines.

The Diabetes Challenge

Diabetes is one of India's most common lifestyle diseases.

Many people with diabetes believe they cannot obtain health insurance.

This is not true.

The key issue is disclosure and timing.

People who purchase coverage before complications develop often have more options than those who delay for many years.

Case Study: Two Different Approaches

Rohit was diagnosed with diabetes at age 40 and purchased health insurance immediately after disclosure.

Vikram delayed insurance planning for eight years.

By the time Vikram applied, additional complications had emerged.

Rohit's journey was significantly smoother because he acted earlier.

The lesson is simple.

Delay increases uncertainty.

Action creates options.

Hypertension and Health Insurance

High blood pressure is another common condition.

Many people ignore it because it feels manageable.

However, hypertension can influence long-term health risk.

Insurers generally want accurate disclosure of:

Diagnosis dates

Medication details

Medical reports

Current control status

Again, transparency is essential.

The Cancer Survivor Question

Many cancer survivors wonder whether health insurance remains available.

The answer depends on several factors:

Type of cancer

Treatment history

Recovery period

Current health status

Insurer guidelines

Every case requires individual evaluation.

The important message is that assumptions should never replace professional assessment.

Apply, disclose, and allow underwriting to determine the outcome.

Why Buying Early Changes Everything

Almost every challenge discussed in this chapter becomes easier when insurance is purchased early.

Younger age.

Fewer medical conditions.

Lower premiums.

Completed waiting periods.

Greater flexibility.

The earlier protection begins, the stronger the long-term foundation becomes.

Advisor Insight

One lesson stands out from years of working with families.

People rarely regret buying health insurance early.

They often regret delaying the decision.

The difference between buying at age 30 and buying at age 50 can be enormous.

Not only financially but also in terms of available options.

Reality Check Exercise

Ask yourself:

Have you disclosed all health conditions?

Do you know your policy waiting periods?

Have you reviewed policy wording?

Would your current policy cover a hospitalization related to an existing condition?

Do you understand your insurer's requirements?

If you cannot answer these questions confidently, your policy deserves a closer review.

Common Mistakes

Hiding medical history.

Ignoring waiting periods.

Purchasing insurance too late.

Assuming every condition receives immediate coverage.

Never reviewing policy documents.

Avoiding medical examinations requested by insurers.

Most claim disputes can be avoided by avoiding these mistakes.

Key Takeaways

Pre-existing diseases must be disclosed honestly.

Waiting periods influence coverage eligibility.

Underwriting helps insurers evaluate risk fairly.

Buying early creates significant advantages.

Medical tests are part of risk assessment.

Transparency improves long-term claim outcomes.

Conclusion

Pre-existing diseases, waiting periods, and underwriting are not obstacles.

They are fundamental components of the health insurance system.

The families that understand these concepts make better decisions, experience fewer surprises, and enjoy stronger protection.

Health insurance is most effective when purchased before problems become serious.

Preparation creates options.

Delay reduces them.

The goal is not merely to obtain a policy.

The goal is to secure long-term financial protection that remains dependable when health challenges arise.

In the next chapter, we will explore one of the most important moments in the insurance journey—the claim process—and learn how to navigate it successfully.

Chapter 9

The Claim: Where Promises Meet Reality

Part I – The Night Everything Depends on a Claim

It was 11:45 p.m. when Mr Shah received the call every family fears.

His wife, Neha, had collapsed at home. Within minutes, she was rushed to a nearby hospital. Doctors suspected a serious neurological condition and immediately recommended admission.

As hospital staff prepared for treatment, Amit stood at the insurance desk clutching his wife's health insurance card.

At that moment, nothing else mattered.

Not investments. Not career goals. Not property. Not retirement planning.

Only one question mattered:

"Will the insurance claim be approved?"

For years, Amit had paid health insurance premiums regularly. Like most policyholders, he never imagined how emotionally important a claim would become.

People often think health insurance is purchased when the policy is issued. The truth is different. Health insurance is truly experienced only when a claim occurs.

That night, Amit discovered what thousands of Indian families discover every day.

The claim is the moment where promises meet reality.

The Waiting Period No One Talks About

The hospital insurance desk informed Amit that the cashless request had been submitted.

Now they had to wait.

Five minutes felt like thirty. Thirty minutes felt like three hours.

Every phone call created hope. Every delay created anxiety.

Most policyholders imagine claims as simple administrative processes. In reality, claims occur during emotionally charged moments.

Families are frightened. Patients are vulnerable. Decisions are urgent.

This emotional context is what makes claims so important.

The claim is not merely paperwork. It is peace of mind.

Part II – The Good Claim and the Bad Claim

Story One: The Perfect Claim

Rohit and Priya had maintained their health insurance policy for seven years.

They reviewed coverage annually. They knew their network hospitals. They stored documents digitally.

When Priya required surgery, the claim process moved smoothly.

Cashless approval arrived quickly. Documentation was complete. Hospital coordination was efficient.

The surgery succeeded. The claim settled successfully.

After discharge, Rohit made an interesting observation:

"The claim felt easy because the preparation happened years earlier."

Story Two: The Claim That Should Have Been Approved

Mr. Verma purchased health insurance at age forty-eight.

Several years earlier, he had been diagnosed with diabetes. Fearing higher premiums, he chose not to disclose the condition.

Years later, hospitalization became necessary.

During claim evaluation, earlier medical records revealed the undisclosed history.

The family felt shocked.

The insurer referred to policy disclosures.

The issue was not diabetes.

The issue was non-disclosure.

This case illustrates one of the most important principles in insurance.

The best claim strategy begins with honesty.

Part III – Claim Mastery Framework

Understanding the Players

A successful claim often involves several parties.

The patient. The family. The hospital. The insurer. The TPA (if applicable).

Each plays a role.

Understanding these relationships reduces confusion.

Advisor's Corner

Throughout my career in financial services and insurance, I have observed one powerful pattern.

Families rarely remember the premium they paid.

They remember the claim experience.

They remember whether help arrived when needed.

The strongest policy is not always the cheapest.

The strongest policy is the one that performs when the family needs it most.

Final Lesson

Health insurance is purchased with money.

Its value is measured in confidence.

The claim is not merely a transaction.

It is a test of preparation, understanding, and whether the protection strategy actually works.

When the claim works, families gain something more valuable than reimbursement.

They gain peace of mind.

Chapter 10

Super Top-Up Plans, Riders and Critical Illness Cover

Introduction

A common mistake many families make is believing that a standard health insurance policy is enough to protect them against every medical emergency.

Years ago, a ₹ 5 lakh. policy may have provided strong protection. Today, rising healthcare costs, expensive surgeries, advanced treatments, and long-term illnesses have changed the situation dramatically.

This is where Super Top-Up Plans, Riders, and Critical Illness Covers become important.

Think of health insurance as the foundation of a house.

A foundation is essential.

However, as risks increase, additional layers of protection become necessary.

These advanced protection tools help strengthen your healthcare safety net and reduce the risk of a major medical event destroying years of financial progress.

Why Basic Health Insurance May Not Be Enough

Healthcare inflation continues to rise.

Cancer treatment can cost several lakhs.

Cardiac procedures can cost several lakhs.

Organ transplants, prolonged ICU admissions, and advanced therapies can create very large medical bills.

Many families discover that their standard health insurance policy provides useful support but may not be sufficient for every situation.

This does not mean basic health insurance is inadequate.

It means healthcare risks have evolved.

Protection strategies must evolve too.

The Layered Protection Philosophy

Imagine driving a car.

You use seat belts.

You have airbags.

You follow traffic rules.

You maintain insurance.

Each layer performs a different function.

Health insurance planning works similarly.

Layer One:

Base Health Insurance.

Layer Two:

Super Top-Up Coverage.

Layer Three:

Critical Illness Protection.

Layer Four:

Emergency Savings.

The objective is not to rely on a single solution.

The objective is to build multiple layers of financial protection.

What Is a Top-Up Plan?

A top-up plan provides additional protection above a specified threshold.

For example:

Suppose a top-up policy has a deductible of ₹ 5 lakh..

Claims above that amount may become eligible according to policy terms.

Top-up plans help increase overall protection without significantly increasing premiums.

However, top-up plans and super top-up plans are not identical.

Understanding the difference is important.

What Is a Super Top-Up Plan?

A super top-up plan also works above a deductible.

The key difference lies in how claims are calculated.

A standard top-up may evaluate claims individually.

A super top-up generally considers cumulative medical expenses according to policy conditions.

This distinction can become very valuable when multiple hospitalizations occur within a policy year.

Many experienced advisors consider super top-up plans among the most cost-effective protection tools available.

Case Study: The Power of a Super Top-Up

Mr. Patel had:

₹10 lakh. base policy.

40 lakh super top-up.

Initially he questioned whether additional coverage was necessary.

Several years later, a serious medical condition resulted in substantial treatment costs.

The combination of base coverage and super top-up protection created significantly stronger financial security than the base policy alone.

The lesson was simple.

Large medical events are rare.

But when they occur, additional protection becomes invaluable.

Why Super Top-Ups Are Growing in Popularity

Three reasons explain their popularity.

First, healthcare costs are increasing.

Second, families want higher protection.

Third, super top-ups often provide large coverage amounts at relatively affordable premiums.

This combination makes them attractive for many households.

The Critical Illness Challenge

Not all medical risks look the same.

Traditional health insurance generally focuses on hospitalization expenses.

Critical illnesses create a different financial challenge.

A serious illness may affect:

Income.

Lifestyle.

Business operations.

Retirement plans.

Family goals.

Even when hospitalization expenses are covered, other financial consequences may continue.

This is where critical illness protection becomes important.

What Is Critical Illness Insurance?

Critical illness coverage generally provides a lump-sum benefit upon diagnosis of specified illnesses according to policy terms.

Examples:-

Cancer.

Heart attack.

Stroke.

Major organ failure.

Certain neurological conditions.

The benefit structure differs from traditional hospitalization reimbursement.

The objective is broader financial support.

A Family has:

₹10 lakh. base plan

50 lakh super top-up

Cancer treatment

3 ₹ 5 lakh. bill

Family survives financially, get cover ₹10 lakh. from basic policy and 2 ₹ 5 lakh. from Super top up policy.

Why Critical Illness Cover Matters

Consider a business owner diagnosed with cancer.

Hospital expenses represent only part of the challenge.

The business may suffer.

Income may decline.

Recovery may require months away from work.

Additional lifestyle expenses may emerge.

A lump-sum benefit can help address these broader financial consequences.

Case Study: The Business Owner

Mr. Mehra owned a successful business.

A serious illness forced him to reduce working hours for several months.

His health insurance covered hospitalization expenses.

However, income disruption created additional pressure.

A critical illness benefit provided financial flexibility during recovery.

This illustrates why healthcare planning should consider more than hospital bills alone.

The Difference Between Health Insurance and Critical Illness Cover

Health Insurance

Pays eligible medical expenses according to policy conditions.

Critical Illness Cover

Provides a defined lump-sum benefit after diagnosis of covered illnesses according to policy terms.

The two products serve different purposes.

One focuses primarily on treatment costs.

The other addresses broader financial impact.

Why Riders Exist

Insurance companies often offer optional riders.

A rider is an additional benefit attached to a base policy.

Riders help customize protection.

Examples may include:

Critical illness benefits.

Hospital cash benefits.

Personal accident protection.

Additional health-related benefits.

Not every rider is necessary.

However, the right rider can strengthen a protection strategy.

Choosing Riders Wisely

Many customers automatically select every available rider.

Others reject all riders.

Neither approach is ideal.

The objective is relevance.

Ask:

What risks concern the family most?

What protection gaps currently exist?

Which benefits provide meaningful value?

The answers guide better decisions.

The Affordability Question

Many people assume stronger protection automatically means unaffordable premiums.

This is not always true.

A carefully structured combination of:

Base Health Insurance.

Super Top-Up.

Selected Riders.

may provide excellent protection at reasonable cost.

Smart planning often creates better outcomes than simply purchasing the largest base policy available.

The Role of Inflation

Healthcare inflation affects every protection decision.

A coverage amount that feels comfortable today may feel inadequate ten years later.

This is why periodic review is important.

Families should regularly evaluate:

Coverage amounts.

Protection layers.

Financial goals.

Healthcare risks.

Review creates relevance.

Advisor Insight

Throughout my insurance career, one pattern has remained consistent.

Families regret inadequate protection far more often than they regret having too much protection.

Medical emergencies rarely provide advance notice.

Preparation must occur beforehand.

Super top-ups and critical illness protection exist because modern healthcare risks can exceed traditional coverage assumptions.

Reality Check Exercise

Ask yourself:

Would your current health insurance cover a 2 ₹ 5 lakh. medical event?

What would happen if income stopped for six months?

Would retirement goals remain intact?

Would children's education plans be affected?

Do you have any critical illness protection?

The answers reveal the strength of your current strategy.

Common Mistakes

Relying only on base health insurance.

Ignoring healthcare inflation.

Assuming employer coverage is sufficient.

Never reviewing coverage.

Buying protection without understanding policy terms.

Avoiding these mistakes significantly improves financial resilience.

Key Takeaways

Base health insurance is essential but may not always be sufficient.

Super top-up plans provide additional protection cost-effectively.

Critical illness cover addresses broader financial consequences.

Riders help customize protection.

Healthcare planning should use multiple layers.

Regular reviews keep protection aligned with changing needs.

Conclusion

Health insurance planning is no longer about purchasing a single policy.

It is about creating a protection ecosystem.

Base coverage provides the foundation.

Super top-ups strengthen capacity.

Critical illness benefits address broader financial risks.

Together they create a more resilient financial structure.

The goal is not merely surviving a medical emergency.

The goal is protecting your family's future while navigating it.

In the next chapter, we will focus on business owners and entrepreneurs and explore how healthcare risks affect those who do not have the security of a traditional employer-sponsored afety net.

Chapter 11

The Business Owner Protection Playbook: Protecting the Person Behind the Business

Introduction

Most financial planning advice is written for salaried employees. Business owners live in a different reality.

When a salaried employee falls ill, income may continue through salary, leave balances, or employer support. When a business owner falls ill, revenue, customer relationships, operations, and growth can all be affected simultaneously.

After more than twenty-five years in banking, life insurance, health insurance, and financial services, I have worked with insurance advisors, mutual fund distributors, chartered accountants, traders, shop owners, manufacturers, and entrepreneurs. One lesson appears repeatedly:

The greatest risk to a business is often not competition, inflation, or market conditions.

It is the sudden inability of the owner to work

Story 1: The Insurance Advisor Who Protected Everyone Except Himself

Mahesh had spent nearly twenty years helping families buy insurance.

He explained risk management every day.

He advised clients to disclose medical history honestly.

He encouraged them to review policies annually.

Ironically, he neglected his own protection.

Most of his income was reinvested into business growth. He believed he would review his personal insurance "next year."

At age forty-nine, he suffered a serious cardiac event.

The surgery was successful.

The recovery was long.

For almost four months, client meetings stopped. New business declined sharply. While renewal income continued, fresh revenue almost disappeared.

The hospital bill was painful.

The loss of business momentum was even more painful.

Months later he admitted:

"I spent years protecting my clients. I forgot to protect the person running my business."

Story 2: The Mutual Fund Distributor and the Hidden Cost of Illness

A successful mutual fund distributor had built a practice serving hundreds of families.

His SIP book generated stable income.

His reputation was strong.

Then he was diagnosed with cancer.

The treatment plan lasted nearly a year.

The medical expenses were substantial, but manageable.

What surprised him was the hidden cost.

Client acquisition stopped.

Seminars stopped.

Business expansion stopped.

The opportunity cost became larger than the hospital bill.

Years later he said:

"The treatment cost money. The illness cost growth."

The Real Business Risk

Most entrepreneurs focus on:

Revenue growth.

Profitability.

Customer acquisition.

Tax planning.

Investment planning.

Few focus on continuity planning.

Yet every business depends on certain critical assets.

For many small and medium businesses, the most important asset is the owner.

Without the owner, many decisions stop.

Without decisions, growth stops.

Without growth, financial goals suffer.

Story 3: The Chartered Accountant During Tax Season

A chartered accountant built his practice over fifteen years.

Tax season was his busiest and most profitable period.

During one such season, he experienced a serious health issue requiring hospitalization.

Suddenly, deadlines became impossible.

Clients became anxious.

Work had to be delegated quickly.

Some assignments were postponed.

Some opportunities were lost.

The hospital bill was only one part of the story.

Lost productivity created a second financial impact.

The lesson was simple:

A professional practice is often directly linked to the health of the professional.

Story 4: The Retail Shop Owner

A retail shop owner had built a loyal customer base over two decades.

Customers trusted him personally.

His presence mattered.

When kidney-related complications required repeated treatment, he spent weeks away from the shop.

Sales declined.

Customer engagement weakened.

Operations suffered.

The family had insurance for part of the treatment expenses, but they had never planned for business disruption.

Recovery required more than medical treatment.

It required rebuilding business momentum.

Story 5: The Small Manufacturer

A manufacturing entrepreneur constantly reinvested profits into machinery, inventory, and expansion.

Personal protection was never a priority.

His view was simple:

"The business comes first."

Then a major hospitalization changed everything.

Because protection was inadequate, investments intended for expansion had to be liquidated.

Growth plans stopped.

Cash flow tightened.

The illness did not destroy the business.

Poor preparation almost did.

The Business Continuity Question

Every entrepreneur should answer this question honestly:

If I cannot work for ninety days, what happens?

What happens to revenue?

What happens to employees?

What happens to customers?

What happens to family income?

What happens to loan repayments?

The answers often reveal risks that have never been considered.

The Three Layers of Business Owner Protection

Layer One: Health Insurance

Adequate base health insurance protects against hospitalization expenses.

Layer Two: Super Top-Up Protection

Healthcare inflation continues rising. Additional protection provides a valuable second line of defense.

Layer Three: Emergency Fund

A business owner needs liquidity.

Medical expenses are one challenge.

Income disruption is another.

An emergency fund helps address both.

Why Business Owners Often Need Higher Coverage

Business owners face unique risks:

Income may fluctuate.

There may be no employer benefits.

Family income may depend on one individual.

Business growth may depend on the owner's decisions.

Time away from work can have long-term consequences.

For these reasons, entrepreneurs should often evaluate higher levels of protection than the average salaried employee.

Lessons from 25+ Years in Financial Services

Over the years, I have observed several patterns.

The most successful entrepreneurs are not always the highest earners.

They are often the most prepared.

They understand risk.

They maintain adequate insurance.

They review protection regularly.

They prepare for events they hope never occur.

Preparation creates flexibility.

Flexibility creates resilience.

The Business Owner Protection Checklist

Do I have personal health insurance?

Is my coverage adequate for today's healthcare costs?

Do I have a super top-up plan?

Could my family survive six months without my active involvement?

Are business loans properly planned for?

Do key family members know where policy documents are stored?

Have I reviewed my protection within the last year?

Every “No” represents an opportunity for improvement.

Final Reflection

One entrepreneur shared a lesson I never forgot:

“I insured my factory. I insured my vehicles. I insured my inventory. I forgot to insure my ability to keep everything running.”

That statement captures the essence of this chapter.

Conclusion

Business owners spend years building enterprises, serving customers, supporting employees, and creating opportunities.

But behind every successful business stands a human being.

When that person suffers a health crisis, the effects often extend far beyond hospital bills.

Healthcare planning is not merely personal planning.

It is business continuity planning.

The strongest businesses are built on strong foundations.

And one of the most important foundations is protecting the person who makes everything possible.

Chapter 12

Your 90-Day Health Protection Action Plan

Introduction

Knowledge is valuable, but knowledge alone does not create protection.

Throughout this book, we have explored the financial risks associated with healthcare, the importance of health insurance, claim management, policy structures, critical illness planning, and business continuity.

Now it is time to move from understanding to action.

Many families know they should improve their healthcare planning. The challenge is that they never create a structured plan.

This chapter provides a practical 90-day roadmap designed to help readers strengthen their family's healthcare security step by step.

The objective is simple.

At the end of ninety days, you should be significantly better prepared than you are today.

Why Most Families Never Take Action

People delay healthcare planning for many reasons.

They are busy.

They feel healthy.

They assume there is still time.

They believe medical emergencies happen to others.

Unfortunately, health events rarely arrive with advance notice.

Preparation must happen before the crisis.

The purpose of this action plan is to create momentum.

Small actions completed consistently can dramatically improve financial protection.

The 90-Day Framework

The plan is divided into three phases.

Days 1–30:

Awareness and Assessment.

Days 31–60:

Protection and Implementation.

Days 61–90:

Optimization and Long-Term Planning.

Each phase builds upon the previous one.

Phase One: Awareness and Assessment

The first thirty days focus on understanding your current position.

You cannot improve what you have not evaluated.

Week One: Gather Information

Collect:

Health insurance policies.

Employer coverage details.

Family medical history.

Emergency fund information.

Investment records related to healthcare planning.

Create a single folder—physical or digital—for healthcare documents.

Many families waste valuable time during emergencies because documents are scattered.

Week Two: Coverage Review

Review:

Coverage amounts.

Waiting periods.

Policy renewals.

Network hospitals.

Co-payment clauses.

Exclusions.

Do not assume you know your policy.

Verify it.

Week Three: Family Discussion

Most healthcare planning happens individually.

It should happen collectively.

Discuss:

Current coverage.

Emergency contacts.

Hospital preferences.

Financial responsibilities.

Medical history.

The goal is to ensure that family members know what to do during an emergency.

Week Four: Risk Assessment

Ask:

What would happen if hospitalization occurred tomorrow?

How much coverage exists?

Would savings be sufficient?

Would investments be affected?

Would income disruption create challenges?

This exercise identifies protection gaps.

Phase Two: Protection and Implementation

Once awareness is established, action becomes easier.

Week Five: Upgrade Protection

Evaluate whether current health insurance remains adequate.

Healthcare inflation may have reduced the effectiveness of older coverage levels.

Consider:

Additional coverage.

Super top-up plans.

Family protection improvements.

Parent protection reviews.

The objective is stronger protection aligned with current realities.

Week Six: Parent Protection Audit

Parents often represent the most overlooked area of healthcare planning.

Review:

Existing policies.

Coverage adequacy.

Waiting periods.

Renewal status.

Senior citizen protection needs.

Many families discover gaps during this stage.

Week Seven: Emergency Fund Creation

Health insurance is essential.

Emergency funds remain important.

Create a target emergency reserve dedicated to healthcare-related contingencies.

The exact amount varies by family circumstances.

The objective is immediate liquidity.

Week Eight: Network Hospital Verification

Identify:

Nearest network hospitals.

Preferred hospitals.

Specialized treatment facilities.

Emergency care options.

Knowing this information before a crisis reduces confusion later.

Phase Three: Optimization and Long-Term Planning

The final thirty days focus on strengthening and maintaining the system.

Week Nine: Documentation System

Create an organized healthcare file containing:

Policy documents.

Identity documents.

Medical records.

Claim forms.

Emergency contacts.

Hospital information.

Accessibility is important.

Family members should know where these records are stored.

Week Ten: Preventive Healthcare Planning

Schedule:

Annual health check-ups.

Screenings.

Preventive consultations.

Lifestyle reviews.

The most affordable healthcare strategy is prevention.

Early detection frequently reduces long-term costs.

Week Eleven: Family Healthcare Calendar

Create reminders for:

Policy renewals.

Health check-ups.

Medical reviews.

Coverage reviews.

Important healthcare deadlines.

Consistency matters more than complexity.

Week Twelve: Long-Term Strategy

Review:

Coverage adequacy.

Financial goals.

Healthcare inflation.

Retirement healthcare planning.

Family responsibilities.

The objective is sustainability.

Protection should evolve as life evolves.

The Family Protection Scorecard

Rate yourself from one to five in each category.

Health Insurance Coverage.

Emergency Fund.

Parent Protection.

Critical Illness Protection.

Document Organization.

Hospital Awareness.

Family Preparedness.

A lower score identifies areas requiring attention.

Case Study: The Family That Prepared

The Joshi family spent three months improving healthcare planning.

They reviewed policies.

Built emergency reserves.

Updated coverage.

Organized documentation.

Discussed emergency procedures.

Six months later, an unexpected hospitalization occurred.

Although the experience was stressful, they avoided financial panic.

Preparation created confidence.

Preparation created options.

The Power of Small Improvements

Many people believe financial protection requires major changes.

This is not always true.

Small improvements can create significant results.

Increasing coverage.

Organizing documents.

Completing health check-ups.

Reviewing policy wording.

Building emergency reserves.

Each action strengthens resilience.

Advisor Insight

Throughout my career, I have observed a simple truth.

Families who prepare before emergencies perform better during emergencies.

Preparation does not eliminate uncertainty.

It reduces vulnerability.

Healthcare planning should not begin at hospital admission.

It should begin years earlier.

The 90-day framework exists because action is easier when broken into manageable steps.

Reality Check Exercise

Can your family locate every health insurance policy today?

Do family members know whom to call during a hospitalization?

Are parents adequately protected?

Would a major hospitalization affect education goals?

Is your emergency fund sufficient?

Would your current strategy survive a prolonged illness?

Honest answers reveal preparedness.

Common Mistakes

Postponing healthcare planning.

Never reviewing policies.

Ignoring parents' protection needs.

Assuming employer insurance is enough.

Failing to organize documentation.

Avoiding family discussions.

Most of these mistakes are easily correctable.

Key Takeaways

Knowledge without action creates no protection.

The first thirty days focus on assessment.

The second thirty days focus on implementation.

The final thirty days focus on optimization.

Family involvement is essential.

Healthcare planning should become a recurring habit.

Small actions create powerful results.

Conclusion

The purpose of this book is not merely to increase awareness.

The purpose is to create action.

A medical emergency may arrive unexpectedly.

Financial preparation should not.

The families who begin planning today place themselves in a stronger position tomorrow.

Ninety days may not seem significant.

Yet ninety days of focused action can dramatically improve healthcare security, financial resilience, and peace of mind.

Protection is not created in a single decision.

It is created through consistent action over time.

In the next chapter, we will examine the most common health insurance mistakes that push families toward financial hardship and learn how to avoid them.

Chapter 13

10 Health Insurance Mistakes That Push Families Into Poverty

Introduction

Most financial disasters are not caused by a single mistake.

They are caused by a series of small mistakes that remain unnoticed until a crisis occurs.

Healthcare-related financial problems often follow the same pattern.

Families work hard, save regularly, invest wisely, and plan for the future. Yet one medical emergency can erase years of progress when critical protection mistakes are ignored.

The purpose of this chapter is not to create fear.

The purpose is to create awareness.

Over the years, I have seen certain mistakes repeated again and again by families from different income groups, professions, and backgrounds.

Some mistakes appear harmless.

Others seem logical at the time.

Yet when a hospitalization occurs, their consequences

become painfully clear.

Let us examine the ten most common mistakes that push families toward financial hardship and learn how to avoid them.

Mistake #1 – Buying Health Insurance Too Late

The most expensive health insurance decision is often waiting.

Many people delay buying coverage because they are young and healthy.

Others believe they can purchase insurance later.

Unfortunately, health conditions do not always provide advance warning.

As age increases, premiums rise.

Medical conditions become more common.

Policy options may become limited.

Waiting periods become more relevant.

Buying early provides advantages that cannot always be recreated later.

The lesson is simple.

Buy health insurance before you need it.

Mistake #2 – Depending Only on Employer Insurance

Employer health insurance is valuable.

However, it is not permanent.

Job changes occur.

Companies change policies.

Retirement eventually arrives.

Families that depend entirely on employer coverage often discover protection gaps at the worst possible time.

Corporate insurance should be viewed as one layer of protection, not the entire strategy.

Mistake #3 – Choosing the Cheapest Policy

Many buyers compare only premiums.

They assume all policies are similar.

They are not.

A low-cost policy may contain:

Coverage restrictions.

Higher co-payments.

Sub-limits.

Limited benefits.

Fewer features.

Price matters.

Protection matters more.

The objective is value—not merely affordability.

Mistake #4 – Hiding Medical History

This is one of the most dangerous mistakes.

Some individuals fear higher premiums and therefore fail to disclose existing medical conditions.

Others believe minor illnesses are irrelevant.

During a claim, medical records frequently reveal earlier diagnoses.

The result can be delays, complications, or disputes.

Transparency creates trust.

Trust improves outcomes.

Honest disclosure is always the better strategy.

Mistake #5 – Ignoring Waiting Periods

Many policyholders purchase coverage without understanding waiting periods.

Later they discover that certain conditions are not immediately covered.

This creates frustration and disappointment.

Waiting periods are fundamental to health insurance.

Understanding them before purchase prevents unrealistic expectations.

Mistake #6 – Being Underinsured

A family may have insurance and still face financial stress.

Why?

Because the coverage amount is too small.

Healthcare inflation continues increasing.

Major treatments can cost several lakhs.

Coverage that seemed adequate years ago may no longer provide sufficient protection.

Underinsurance is one of the most common forms of financial vulnerability.

Regular reviews are essential.

Mistake #7 – Ignoring Parents' Healthcare Planning

Many families focus exclusively on themselves and their children.

Parents receive less attention.

Unfortunately, healthcare utilization generally increases with age.

A parent's medical emergency can create substantial financial pressure if protection is inadequate.

Parents deserve their own healthcare strategy.

Ignoring this responsibility often becomes expensive.

Mistake #8 – Missing Renewals

Health insurance is most valuable when continuity is maintained.

Allowing a policy to lapse can create multiple problems.

Coverage interruption.

Loss of continuity benefits.

Waiting period implications.

Reduced protection.

A missed renewal may appear minor.

Its consequences can be significant.

Every family should maintain a reliable renewal reminder system.

Mistake #9 – Never Learning the Claim Process

Many people spend years paying premiums without understanding how claims work.

Then a hospitalization occurs.

Suddenly they must learn everything under pressure.

Policyholders should understand:

Cashless claims.

Reimbursement claims.

Documentation requirements.

Network hospitals.

Escalation procedures.

Preparation improves confidence.

Confidence improves outcomes.

Mistake #10 – Never Reviewing the Policy

Life changes.

Marriage.

Children.

Income growth.

Relocation.

Healthcare inflation.

Yet many families continue with the same policy year after year without review.

Protection that was appropriate five years ago may be inadequate today.

Insurance should evolve alongside life.

Case Study: The Perfect Storm

The Sharma family made several small mistakes simultaneously.

Coverage was too low.

Parents were uninsured.

Employer coverage created false confidence.

Policies were rarely reviewed.

When a major medical emergency occurred, every weakness became visible.

No single mistake caused the problem.

The combination created the crisis.

This illustrates an important lesson.

Financial vulnerability often develops gradually.

The Cost of Ignoring Small Problems

Most healthcare planning mistakes seem minor in isolation.

A delayed review.

A missed disclosure.

An insufficient sum insured.

A postponed purchase.

Individually they may appear manageable.

Collectively they create risk.

Good financial planning is often the result of addressing small issues before they become large problems.

The Psychology Behind These Mistakes

Why do intelligent people make these mistakes?

Optimism.

Procrastination.

Overconfidence.

Complexity.

Competing financial priorities.

Human beings naturally focus on immediate concerns.

Healthcare planning often feels less urgent until a medical event occurs.

The challenge is acting before urgency arrives.

Advisor Insight

Throughout my professional journey, I have observed a powerful pattern.

Families rarely regret being prepared.

They frequently regret delaying preparation.

The cost of planning is usually small.

The cost of neglect can be enormous.

Most healthcare-related financial crises are not caused by bad luck alone.

They are amplified by preventable mistakes.

Reality Check Exercise

Ask yourself:

Did I buy health insurance early?

Am I dependent on employer coverage?

Do I understand my policy conditions?

Have I disclosed all health conditions?

Are my parents adequately protected?

Is my coverage amount still sufficient?

Do I know my claim process?

Have I reviewed my policy within the last year?

Your answers reveal where improvement is needed.

The Prevention Strategy

Avoiding these mistakes does not require advanced financial knowledge.

It requires discipline.

Buy early.

Review regularly.

Disclose honestly.

Maintain continuity.

Protect parents.

Understand claims.

Upgrade coverage when necessary.

Simple actions create powerful results.

Key Takeaways

Most healthcare-related financial disasters are preventable.

Buying late increases risk.

Employer coverage alone is insufficient.

The cheapest policy is not always the best policy.

Honest disclosure matters.

Coverage should be reviewed regularly.

Parents require dedicated attention.

Claims should be understood before emergencies occur.

Conclusion

Financial protection is not created by luck.

It is created by preparation.

The ten mistakes discussed in this chapter appear

repeatedly because they are easy to make and easy to ignore.

Yet they are also avoidable.

Families that learn from these mistakes place themselves in a stronger position than families who repeat them.

The goal of health insurance is not merely paying hospital bills.

The goal is protecting the dreams, goals, savings, and future that families spend years building.

In the next chapter, we will create a complete Annual Health Insurance Review Checklist that readers can use every year to ensure their protection remains strong, relevant, and effective.

Chapter 14

The Annual Health Insurance Review Checklist

Introduction

Most families review their investments every year.

They check mutual funds.

They monitor bank balances.

They evaluate property values.

Yet very few families review their health insurance with the same seriousness.

This is surprising because a health insurance policy is one of the most important financial protection tools a family owns.

A policy purchased five years ago may not be suitable today.

Family circumstances change.

Healthcare costs change.

Income changes.

Responsibilities change.

Health insurance should evolve accordingly.

The purpose of this chapter is to provide a practical annual review framework that helps families ensure their protection remains relevant, adequate, and effective.

Why Annual Reviews Matter

Imagine buying a shirt for a ten-year-old child and expecting it to fit perfectly ten years later.

Life changes.

Needs change.

Protection requirements change.

The same principle applies to health insurance.

Annual reviews help identify gaps before those gaps become expensive problems.

A policy should not be reviewed only during claims.

It should be reviewed proactively every year.

The Annual Health Insurance Review Philosophy

A strong review process answers four questions.

Do we have enough coverage?

Do we have the right structure?

Do we understand our policies?

Would our protection work if hospitalization occurred tomorrow?

If the answer to any of these questions is uncertain, a review is necessary.

Step One: Review Coverage Amounts

The first task is evaluating coverage adequacy.

Ask:

Would current coverage handle a major hospitalization?

Would it remain sufficient after healthcare inflation?

Would it cover treatment in a quality hospital?

Many families continue with coverage amounts selected years earlier.

Healthcare costs have increased dramatically.

Coverage should reflect current realities—not past assumptions.

The Healthcare Inflation Test

A simple exercise is useful.

Imagine your largest expected medical expense.

Now assume healthcare costs double over the next decade.

Would your current coverage remain adequate?

If the answer is no, additional protection may be necessary.

Step Two: Review Family Changes

Life evolves continuously.

Marriage.

Children.

Parents aging.

Career growth.

Business expansion.

Relocation.

Each change influences healthcare planning.

The protection structure should evolve alongside family circumstances.

Coverage that worked for a young couple may not be sufficient for a family with children and aging parents.

Step Three: Parent Protection Review

Parents deserve special attention during annual reviews.

Questions to ask:

Do parents have active policies?

Is coverage adequate?

Have premiums changed significantly?

Are policy renewals current?

Have healthcare needs increased?

Many families discover protection gaps only after a parent's hospitalization.

Annual reviews help prevent surprises.

Step Four: Employer Coverage Assessment

Employees often assume corporate insurance is enough.

Annual reviews should examine:

Coverage amount.

Dependent eligibility.

Policy changes.

Potential gaps.

Remember:

Employer insurance is valuable.

However, personal protection remains essential.

Step Five: Policy Structure Review

Evaluate whether the current structure still makes sense.

Family Floater?

Individual Policies?

Super Top-Up?

Critical Illness Cover?

The objective is ensuring the protection framework remains aligned with family needs.

Step Six: Waiting Period Status

Many policyholders forget about waiting periods after purchase.

Annual reviews should confirm:

Which waiting periods have been completed?

Which conditions remain subject to restrictions?

What benefits are now fully available?

This information becomes valuable during future claims.

Step Seven: Network Hospital Verification

Hospital networks change over time.

A hospital available today may not remain available indefinitely.

Review:

Nearby network hospitals.

Preferred hospitals.

Specialized facilities.

Emergency options.

Access matters.

Protection is most valuable when it is convenient to use.

Step Eight: Claim Readiness Assessment

Ask:

Can policy documents be located quickly?

Are family members aware of procedures?

Do emergency contacts exist?

Are claim documents organized?

Many claim challenges result from poor preparation rather than poor coverage.

Claim readiness should be reviewed annually.

The Family Healthcare File

Every family should maintain a healthcare file.

Contents may include:

Policy documents.

Health cards.

Medical reports.

Claim forms.

Emergency contacts.

Hospital information.

Doctor contact details.

Accessibility is critical.

Information should be available when needed—not searched for during emergencies.

Case Study: The Annual Review Advantage

The Deshpande family reviewed healthcare protection every year.

During one review they discovered:

Coverage was outdated.

Parents required additional protection.

A network hospital had changed.

Several documents were missing.

These issues were corrected before any medical emergency occurred.

Two years later, a major hospitalization happened.

The family handled the situation confidently because preparation had already been completed.

The Cost of Not Reviewing

Many healthcare problems originate from neglect.

Coverage remains unchanged.

Policies are forgotten.

Renewals are missed.

Parents become underinsured.

Inflation reduces protection value.

The cost of an annual review is minimal.

The cost of ignoring one can be enormous.

The Healthcare Audit Scorecard

Rate your family from one to five in each category.

Coverage Adequacy.

Emergency Fund.

Parent Protection.

Claim Readiness.

Document Organization.

Critical Illness Protection.

Policy Understanding.

Hospital Awareness.

Lower scores indicate areas requiring immediate attention.

Advisor Insight

One lesson stands out from years of working with families.

The best healthcare decisions are rarely made during emergencies.

They are made long before emergencies occur.

Annual reviews provide an opportunity to identify weaknesses while there is still time to correct them.

The families who review regularly generally experience fewer surprises and greater confidence.

The Annual Healthcare Calendar

January:

Review coverage amounts.

February:

Update family records.

March:

Review emergency funds.

April:

Verify network hospitals.

May:

Review parent protection.

June:

Check policy documents.

July:

Assess healthcare inflation impact.

August:

Review critical illness protection.

September:

Update medical records.

October:

Conduct family discussion.

November:

Review claims preparedness.

December:

Complete annual healthcare audit.

This simple structure creates consistency.

Reality Check Exercise

Can you answer these questions immediately?

How much health insurance coverage do you currently have?

When is your next renewal?

What hospital would you choose during an emergency?

Do your parents have adequate coverage?

Do family members know claim procedures?

If not, your annual review process may need improvement.

Common Mistakes

Never reviewing policies.

Ignoring healthcare inflation.

Assuming old coverage remains sufficient.

Neglecting parent protection.

Failing to organize documents.

Depending entirely on memory.

Avoiding these mistakes improves preparedness dramatically.

Key Takeaways

Health insurance requires annual review.

Coverage should evolve with life circumstances.

Healthcare inflation affects protection adequacy.

Parents require regular attention.

Claim readiness is important.

Organization improves outcomes.

Small annual reviews prevent large future problems.

Conclusion

Health insurance is not a one-time purchase.

It is an ongoing protection strategy.

The families who benefit most from health insurance are not necessarily those who buy the largest policies.

They are the families who remain engaged, informed, and proactive.

An annual review requires only a few hours.

Yet those few hours can protect years of savings, investments, goals, and financial progress.

The objective is simple.

Ensure that when a healthcare challenge arrives, your family is prepared—not surprised.

With this annual review framework, you now have a practical tool that can be used year after year to maintain strong and effective healthcare protection.

Chapter 15

The Hospitalization Survival Guide

Introduction

A medical emergency creates two battles at the same time.

The first battle is medical.

The second battle is financial and administrative.

Most families focus entirely on treatment, which is understandable. However, confusion, panic, missing documents, poor communication, and billing mistakes can make an already difficult situation even harder.

This chapter is designed as a practical survival guide.

Its purpose is simple: help families navigate hospitalization with confidence, clarity, and control.

The Golden Rule of Hospitalization

During a health crisis, emotions run high.

Fear often replaces logic.

Decisions are made quickly.

Important details are overlooked.

The first rule is simple:

Stay calm and stay organized.

A calm family usually makes better decisions than a panicked family.

The First 60 Minutes

The first hour after hospitalization is often the most important.

Focus on four priorities:

Medical stabilization.

Hospital registration.

Insurance information.

Family communication.

Do not attempt to solve every problem immediately.

Focus on the next necessary step.

Emergency Admission Checklist

Carry or store digitally:

Health insurance card.

Identity proof.

Policy details.

Emergency contacts.

Medical history.

Current medications.

Doctor contact information.

These simple preparations save valuable time.

Choosing the Right Hospital

In an emergency, the nearest hospital may be the right choice.

For planned treatment, however, hospital selection deserves careful consideration.

Evaluate:

Doctor expertise.

Hospital reputation.

Insurance network status.

Distance from home.

Critical care facilities.

A good hospital is not always the most expensive hospital.

Communication With Doctors

Families often feel intimidated during medical discussions.

Remember:

You have the right to understand.

Ask questions.

Request clarification.

Understand diagnosis.

Understand treatment options.

Understand risks and expected outcomes.

Good communication improves decision quality.

The Role of a Family Coordinator

One person should coordinate:

Doctor discussions.

Insurance communication.

Document collection.

Billing review.

Family updates.

When multiple people try to manage everything simultaneously, confusion increases.

A designated coordinator improves efficiency.

Understanding the Daily Bill

Many families wait until discharge to review expenses.

This is a mistake.

Review bills regularly during hospitalization.

Check:

Room charges.

Pharmacy expenses.

Investigations.

Consultation fees.

Consumables.

Early review helps identify discrepancies before discharge.

The Insurance Desk

Every insured patient should connect with the hospital insurance desk as early as possible.

Confirm:

Cashless eligibility.

Documentation requirements.

Approval status.

Policy details.

Communication delays often occur because families engage too late.

How Cashless Claims Work

Cashless hospitalization reduces financial stress.

However, approval depends on:

Policy terms.

Coverage availability.

Documentation.

Medical necessity.

Understand that approval and final settlement may differ.

Remain engaged throughout the process.

What If Cashless Is Not Available?

Do not panic.

Reimbursement claims remain an option in many situations.

The key is documentation.

Preserve:

Bills.

Reports.

Prescriptions.

Discharge documents.

Payment receipts.

Organized records simplify reimbursement.

The ICU Experience

Few situations create more emotional pressure than ICU admission.

Families often experience:

Fear.

Exhaustion.

Financial anxiety.

Information overload.

During ICU situations:

Maintain written notes.

Track doctor updates.

Assign responsibilities.

Avoid making assumptions.

Clarity is essential.

Managing Family Expectations

In major medical situations, relatives often seek updates continuously.

This creates additional pressure.

Designate one spokesperson.

Provide regular updates.

Avoid speculation.

Communicate facts rather than assumptions.

This reduces confusion and stress.

The Discharge Process

Many families rush through discharge formalities.

Take your time.

Review:

Final bill.

Discharge summary.

Medicine prescriptions.

Follow-up instructions.

Claim documentation.

A few extra minutes can prevent future complications.

The Importance of the Discharge Summary

The discharge summary is one of the most important documents.

Verify:

Diagnosis.

Treatment details.

Procedure information.

Dates.

Medical history references.

Errors should be corrected immediately.

Understanding Hospital Bills

Hospital bills can appear complicated.

Typical components include:

Room charges.

Doctor visits.

Diagnostic tests.

Medicines.

Nursing charges.

Equipment usage.

Consumables.

Understanding these categories improves bill review.

Case Study: The Billing Error

A family carefully reviewed its discharge bill.

They discovered duplicate charges for a diagnostic procedure.

The error was corrected before payment.

The lesson:

Review every bill carefully.

Mistakes can occur.

How to Prevent Overcharging

Ask questions.

Review bills daily.

Compare charges with treatments received.

Clarify unfamiliar entries.

Maintain records.

Most hospitals operate professionally, but verification remains important.

The Post-Discharge Period

Hospitalization does not end at discharge.

Recovery may continue for weeks or months.

Focus on:

Medication adherence.

Follow-up appointments.

Lifestyle modifications.

Documentation storage.

Claim completion.

The recovery phase deserves as much attention as hospitalization itself.

The Emotional Recovery Process

Serious illness affects more than physical health.

Patients may experience:

Anxiety.

Fear.

Loss of confidence.

Lifestyle adjustments.

Families may experience emotional exhaustion.

Recovery should address both physical and emotional well-being.

Financial Recovery After Hospitalization

A major medical event may affect:

Savings.

Investments.

Cash flow.

Business operations.

Family plans.

Conduct a financial review after recovery.

Understand what changed and rebuild systematically.

The Hospitalization Preparedness Kit

Every family should maintain:

Insurance documents.

Medical records.

Emergency contacts.

Hospital preferences.

Family instructions.

Digital backups.

Preparedness reduces chaos during emergencies.

Advisor Insight

During my years in the insurance and healthcare ecosystem, I have observed a simple pattern.

Families who prepare before hospitalization handle hospitalization better.

Preparation creates confidence.

Organization reduces stress.

Knowledge improves decisions.

A medical emergency may not be predictable.

Preparation is.

Reality Check Exercise

Can your family answer these questions today?

Which hospital would you choose in an emergency?

Where are your policy documents stored?

Who would coordinate hospitalization?

Do family members understand claim procedures?

Can important records be accessed within five minutes?

If not, preparation should begin immediately.

Key Takeaways

Preparation matters.

Documentation matters.

Communication matters.

Bill verification matters.

Insurance coordination matters.

Recovery planning matters.

The families who prepare before hospitalization generally experience less stress during hospitalization.

Conclusion

A hospital admission is never easy.

However, the experience becomes significantly more manageable when families know what to expect and how to respond.

The objective of this chapter is not merely helping readers survive hospitalization.

It is helping them navigate it intelligently.

When preparation, communication, documentation, and protection work together, families gain something extremely valuable during difficult times:

Control.

And in a crisis, control creates confidence.

Chapter 16

Medical Bankruptcy: The Disease That Doesn't Appear in Medical Reports

Part I – The Day the Numbers Stopped Making Sense

The first thing the doctor said was reassuring.

"The surgery was successful."

For a few moments, the Mehta family felt relief.

After twelve hours of anxiety, endless prayers, and nervous waiting outside the operation theatre, they finally heard the words they desperately wanted to hear.

The patient would survive.

Then someone asked the next question.

"What will the bill be?"

The estimated treatment cost was nearly 22 lakh.

Nobody had expected the number.

The family had prepared mentally for a health crisis.

They had not prepared for a financial crisis.

That is how medical bankruptcy begins.

Not with a court order.
Not with a business failure.
Not with reckless spending.

It begins with illness.

The Bankruptcy Nobody Sees

When people hear the word bankruptcy, they imagine failed businesses and unpaid debts.

Medical bankruptcy looks very different.

It happens quietly.

A fixed deposit disappears.
A retirement corpus gets withdrawn.
A mutual fund portfolio is liquidated.
A property is mortgaged.
Gold jewellery is sold.
Education plans are postponed.

The family survives medically.

But financially, something important has been lost.

The Story of Sunita

Sunita was a school teacher.

Her husband worked for a manufacturing company.

Together they had spent almost twenty years building financial security.

They had a home, investments, a retirement plan, and a college fund for their daughter.

Then Sunita was diagnosed with cancer.

Initially the family focused entirely on treatment.

Doctors.
Hospitals.
Second opinions.
Surgery.
Chemotherapy.
Radiation.

The treatment lasted almost eighteen months.

By the time recovery finally arrived, the family had spent far more than expected.

The family survived.

The finances took years to recover.

Years later Sunita would say:

"The cancer lasted eighteen months. The financial recovery lasted six years."

Why Medical Bankruptcy Is Different

Most financial problems develop gradually.

Medical bankruptcy often develops suddenly.

A family may spend twenty years building wealth.

One diagnosis can challenge everything.

The speed of destruction is what makes healthcare risk unique.

Wealth is usually built slowly.

Medical expenses arrive quickly.

The Organ Transplant Story

Among all healthcare events, few are as financially overwhelming as organ transplantation.

The surgery itself is only one part of the expense.

There are:

Pre-transplant investigations.
Donor-related expenses.

Hospitalization.
Medicines.
Long-term monitoring.
Follow-up treatment.

Many families focus only on the operation.

The reality is much larger.

One family described the experience perfectly:

"We thought we were paying for surgery. We later realized we were paying for an entirely new way of life."

The ICU Reality

Few places create more financial anxiety than an intensive care unit.

Families rarely ask about costs during the first day.

Their only concern is survival.

As days pass, reality begins to emerge.

Daily ICU charges.
Specialist consultations.
Advanced investigations.
Life-support equipment.
Medicines.

The financial pressure grows alongside emotional stress.

Part II – When Illness Destroys More Than Health

The greatest misconception about healthcare costs is believing the hospital bill is the biggest problem.

Often it is not.

The bigger problem is what happens afterward.

The Business Owner

Mr. Patel spent twenty-five years building a successful distribution business.

His relationships drove revenue.

His presence drove growth.

When he suffered a serious cardiac event, the hospitalization lasted only a few weeks.

Recovery lasted much longer.

Customers moved elsewhere.
Growth slowed.
Opportunities disappeared.

The medical expenses were painful.

The business disruption was worse.

The Retirement Dream

A retired couple from Nashik believed their financial planning was complete.

They had retirement savings, fixed deposits, modest investments, and a debt-free home.

Then age-related health conditions began appearing.

First one hospitalization.
Then another.
Then regular treatments.

The challenge was not a single large bill.

The challenge was continuous healthcare spending.

Over time, medical expenses consumed a growing share of retirement income.

The Education Fund Sacrifice

One family maintained a dedicated education corpus for their daughter.

The plan was clear.

Higher education.

Financial independence.
Opportunity.

Then a major medical emergency occurred.

The easiest source of money was the education fund.

The treatment succeeded.

The fund disappeared.

The family rebuilt savings over time.

But the original plan was gone.

The Hidden Costs Nobody Calculates

Most people calculate hospital bills.

Very few calculate:

Travel expenses.
Accommodation.
Caregiver costs.
Income loss.
Special diets.
Follow-up treatment.
Emotional exhaustion.

The actual financial impact is often much larger than the hospital invoice.

Part III – The Lessons Every Family Must Learn

After years in insurance and financial services, I have noticed a pattern.

Families who experience medical bankruptcy rarely believe it will happen to them.

They are responsible people.

Hardworking people.

Disciplined savers.

Good planners.

Yet they underestimate one thing.

Healthcare risk.

The Prevention Formula

Medical bankruptcy cannot always be prevented.

Its impact can often be reduced.

The formula is straightforward:

Adequate health insurance.
Super top-up coverage.

Emergency funds.
Critical illness protection.
Annual policy reviews.
Family healthcare planning.

No single solution is perfect.

Multiple layers create resilience.

Advisor's Corner

Throughout my career, I have met families who lost investments, sold property, borrowed money, delayed retirement, and sacrificed educational goals because of healthcare costs.

Most of these stories shared one common theme.

The illness was unavoidable.

The financial damage was partially preventable.

Preparation would not have eliminated the crisis.

It would have reduced the consequences.

Reality Check

Ask yourself honestly:

Could your family survive a 20 lakh medical event?

Would retirement plans remain intact?
Would children's education goals remain untouched?
Could income stop for six months?
Would assets need to be sold?

The answers reveal financial resilience.

Final Thought

Medical bankruptcy is not a medical condition.

You will never see it on a diagnostic report.

Yet every year it affects thousands of families.

The objective of healthcare planning is not simply paying hospital bills.

It is protecting everything those bills threaten:

Savings.
Investments.
Education.
Retirement.
Dreams.

A medical emergency should challenge a family's health.

It should not destroy their future.

Chapter 17

Building a Financially Bulletproof Family.

Introduction

On a rainy evening in Pune, a family sat together at their dining table discussing the future.

The father talked about retirement.

The mother spoke about their daughter's higher education.

Their son discussed career ambitions.

Everyone was planning for tomorrow.

Yet no one discussed the one event that could destroy every plan they had carefully created.

A medical emergency.

This is the reality for millions of Indian families.

They plan for success.

They rarely plan for disruption.

A financially bulletproof family is not a family that avoids problems.

It is a family that can survive problems without losing everything they have worked so hard to build.

What Does Financially Bulletproof Mean?

Being financially bulletproof does not mean being wealthy.

It means being resilient.

It means that one illness, one hospitalization, one accident, or one unexpected event does not destroy years of effort.

Financial resilience allows families to recover, adapt, and continue moving forward.

The Story of Two Families

Family A earned a high income.

They owned a beautiful home.

Luxury vehicles.

Excellent lifestyles.

Strong social status.

Yet they ignored protection planning.

When a major health crisis arrived, investments were

liquidated, loans increased, and retirement plans were delayed.

Family B earned less.

Their lifestyle was simpler.

However, they maintained emergency funds, health insurance, critical illness protection, and disciplined financial planning.

When a medical emergency occurred, the impact was manageable.

The difference was not income.

The difference was preparation.

The Five Pillars of Financial Security

Pillar One – Emergency Fund

Every family needs liquidity.

Medical emergencies do not wait for investments to mature.

A strong emergency fund provides breathing room during difficult times.

Pillar Two – Health Protection

Health insurance remains one of the most important tools of wealth preservation.

The objective is simple:

A hospital bill should not destroy decades of savings.

Pillar Three – Income Protection

Most families depend on one or two primary earners.

If income stops, financial pressure begins immediately.

Income protection includes:

Emergency savings.

Skill development.

Business continuity planning.

Financial reserves.

Pillar Four – Wealth Creation

Protection alone is not enough.

Families must also build wealth through:

Investments.

Retirement planning.

Asset creation.

Disciplined saving.

Pillar Five – Retirement Security

Healthcare expenses often increase during retirement.

A financially bulletproof family plans for healthcare long before retirement begins.

The Parent Protection Challenge

One of the most overlooked areas of financial planning is parent protection.

Many middle-aged families simultaneously support:

Children.

Parents.

Their own future goals.

This creates financial pressure from multiple directions.

A major medical event involving parents can significantly affect long-term plans if preparation is inadequate.

Why Lifestyle Matters

No financial plan can completely compensate for poor health habits.

Exercise.

Nutrition.

Sleep.

Stress management.

Preventive healthcare.

These habits reduce risk and improve long-term outcomes.

The strongest protection strategy combines financial planning with healthy living.

Advisor's Corner

During my professional journey spanning more than two decades in financial services, insurance, and family financial planning, I have observed a consistent pattern.

The families who recover fastest from crises are rarely the richest.

They are usually the most prepared.

They know where important documents are stored.

They maintain emergency reserves.

They review protection regularly.

They understand that wealth creation and wealth protection must work together.

The Family Protection Blueprint

Every family should answer the following questions:

Do we have adequate health insurance?

Do we have emergency reserves?

Are our parents protected?

Could we survive six months of reduced income?

Do family members know emergency procedures?

Can important documents be accessed immediately?

The answers reveal financial readiness.

Annual Family Protection Meeting

Once every year, families should review:

Insurance coverage.

Emergency funds.

Retirement planning.

Parent healthcare needs.

Investment progress.

Financial goals.

A few hours of review can prevent years of financial stress.

The Legacy Question

Most people think financial planning is about money.

It is actually about legacy.

The opportunities we create for our children.

The dignity we preserve for our parents.

The security we provide for our families.

Money is simply the tool.

The real objective is protection.

Reality Check

Imagine receiving a phone call tonight.

A loved one has been admitted to the hospital.

What happens next?

Do you know where your policies are?

Can treatment begin immediately?

Would financial goals remain intact?

Would panic or preparation guide your decisions?

These questions determine financial resilience.

Final Story

Several years after his father's hospitalization, Rakesh looked back on the experience that had changed his family's financial life.

The hospital bill had been large.

The emotional stress had been overwhelming.

The recovery had taken time.

But one lesson remained clear.

The family survived because they adapted.

They strengthened protection.

They improved planning.

They prepared for uncertainty.

That preparation gave them confidence.

Final Thoughts

Throughout this book, we have explored a powerful truth.

Medical emergencies may be unavoidable.

Financial devastation is often preventable.

The goal is not to eliminate risk.

The goal is to build resilience.

A financially bulletproof family is not protected because life is easy.

It is protected because preparation exists before difficulty arrives.

One hospital bill should never destroy a lifetime of dreams.

One diagnosis should never erase decades of effort.

One emergency should never define a family's future.

Plan early.

Protect wisely.

Review regularly.

And build a future strong enough to withstand life's unexpected challenges.

Hospital Emergency Checklist to be carry at the time of hospitalisation

1) All previous treatement record

2) Insurance Policy

3) Any ID proof issued by Government of India

4) Need to communicate treating doctor for all previous history for better and fast treatement.

A Final Letter From the Author

Dear Reader,

If you have reached this page, I would first like to thank you.

Thank you for investing your time in reading this book.

Thank you for caring about your family's future.

And thank you for taking a subject seriously that most people prefer to ignore until it is too late.

When I started my journey in financial services more than twenty-five years ago, I believed my role was to help people buy insurance.

Over time, I realized that insurance was never the real product.

The real product was peace of mind.

Throughout my career in banking, life insurance, health insurance, and financial planning, I have met thousands of families.

Some were wealthy.

Some were middle class.

Some were just beginning their financial journey.

Despite their differences, they all shared one common dream.

They wanted a better future for their families.

Parents wanted quality education for their children.

Children wanted security for their parents.

Couples wanted a comfortable retirement.

Business owners wanted stability and growth.

Everyone was working hard to build something meaningful.

Yet I also witnessed another reality.

I saw families who spent twenty years building financial security and lost a significant part of it within a few weeks because of a medical emergency.

I saw retirement plans postponed.

I saw education funds depleted.

I saw businesses struggle after the illness of a key family member.

I saw people sell assets they had spent decades creating.

And almost every time, the conversation was the same:

'We never thought this would happen to us.'

The truth is that nobody expects a medical emergency.

Nobody plans for a cancer diagnosis.

Nobody schedules a heart attack.

Nobody prepares emotionally for a late-night phone call from a hospital.

Life can change without warning.

That is exactly why preparation matters.

This book was never written to create fear.

Fear does not protect families.

Knowledge does.

Preparation does.

Action does.

If there is only one lesson I hope you remember from this book, let it be this:

Health insurance is not about hospitals.

It is not about policy documents.

It is not about premiums.

It is not about claim forms.

Health insurance is about protecting dreams.

It is about ensuring that a medical emergency does not destroy your child's education.

It is about protecting your retirement.

It is about preserving your dignity.

It is about giving your family choices when life becomes uncertain.

Most people spend years learning how to earn money.

Far fewer spend time learning how to protect it.

Both are equally important.

Because wealth creation without protection is incomplete.

As you close this book, I encourage you to take a simple step.

Do not wait for the perfect time.

Review your family's protection today.

Review your health insurance.

Review your emergency fund.

Review your parents' healthcare planning.

Review the financial risks that could affect your family's future.

Small actions taken today can prevent enormous stress tomorrow.

I also encourage you to have conversations that many families avoid.

Talk openly about healthcare.

Talk openly about protection.

Talk openly about financial preparedness.

These conversations may feel uncomfortable, but they are acts of love and responsibility.

The strongest families are not those who avoid challenges.

The strongest families are those who prepare for them.

If this book helps even one family avoid financial hardship during a medical crisis, then the effort of writing it will have been worthwhile.

As I conclude, I want to leave you with one final thought.

A hospital bill should never destroy a lifetime of dreams.

A diagnosis should never erase decades of hard work.

A medical emergency should challenge your health—not your future.

Prepare wisely.

Protect diligently.

Review regularly.

And build a future strong enough to withstand life's unexpected challenges.

Family Protection Scorecard

Score yourself:

□ Emergency Fund

□ Health Insurance

□ Super Top-Up

□ Parents Covered

□ Policy Documents Organized
□ Annual Review Done
□ Claim Process Understood
□ Employer Dependency Removed

Scoring:
0–3 = High Risk
4–6 = Moderate Risk
7–8 = Well Protected
Ask question yourself
If your family received a hospital estimate of ₹20 lakh tonight, would your first concern be treatment or money?
The purpose of this book is to make sure the answer is always treatment.
Wishing you and your family good health, financial security, and peace of mind.

With warm regards,

Shailesh Shah

Author
One Bill Away – The Untold Story of India's Healthcare Crisis

www.ingramcontent.com/pod-product-compliance
Lightning Source LLC
LaVergne TN
LVHW100307210926
848480LV00003B/1041
* 9 7 9 8 9 0 5 4 0 7 7 9 6 *